MW01628801

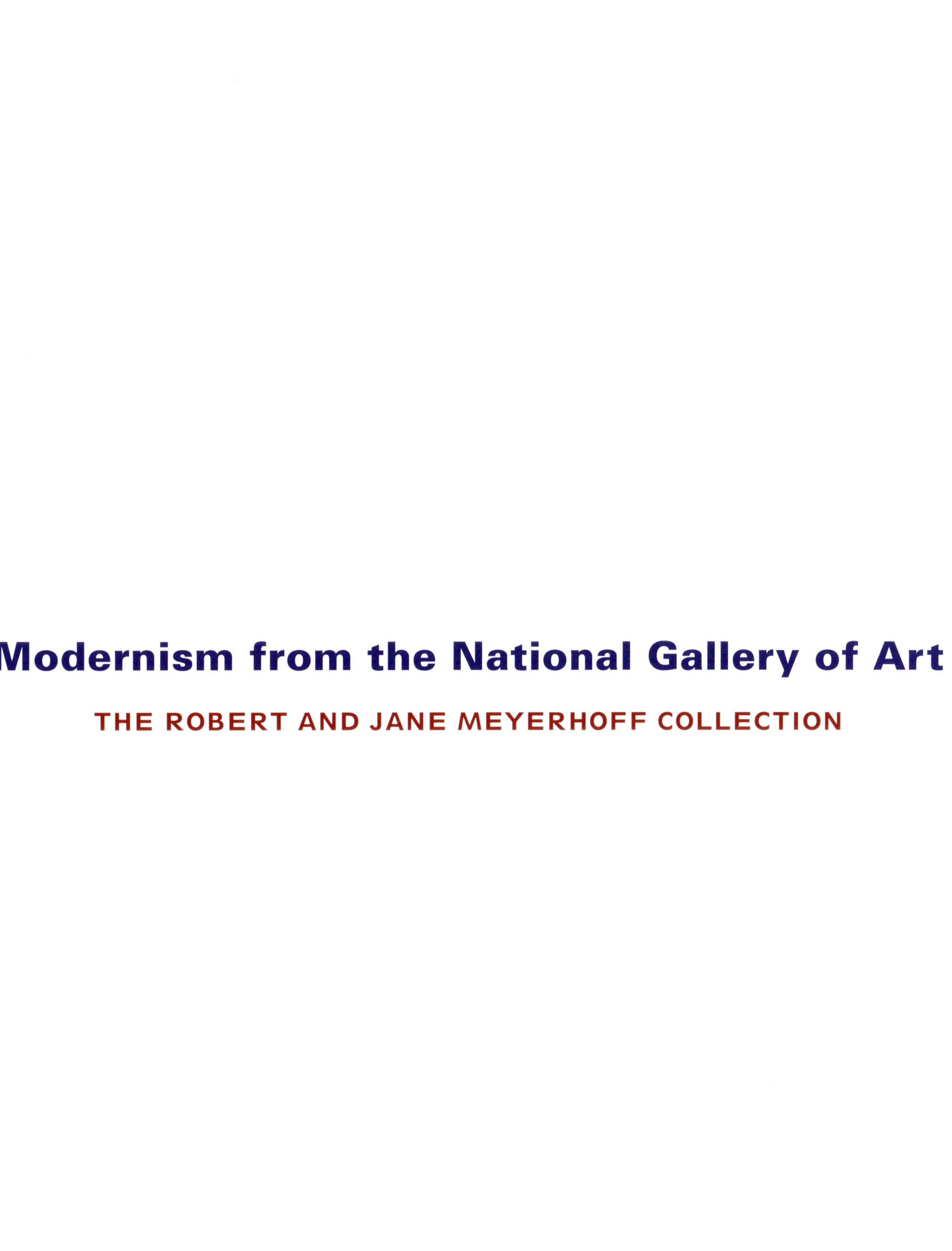

Modernism from the National Gallery of Art

THE ROBERT AND JANE MEYERHOFF COLLECTION

Modernism from the National Gallery of Art

THE ROBERT AND JANE MEYERHOFF COLLECTION

HARRY COOPER

with contributions by Molly Donovan, James Meyer,
Jennifer Roberts, Kerry Rose, and Paige Rozanski

Fine Arts Museums of San Francisco
National Gallery of Art, Washington

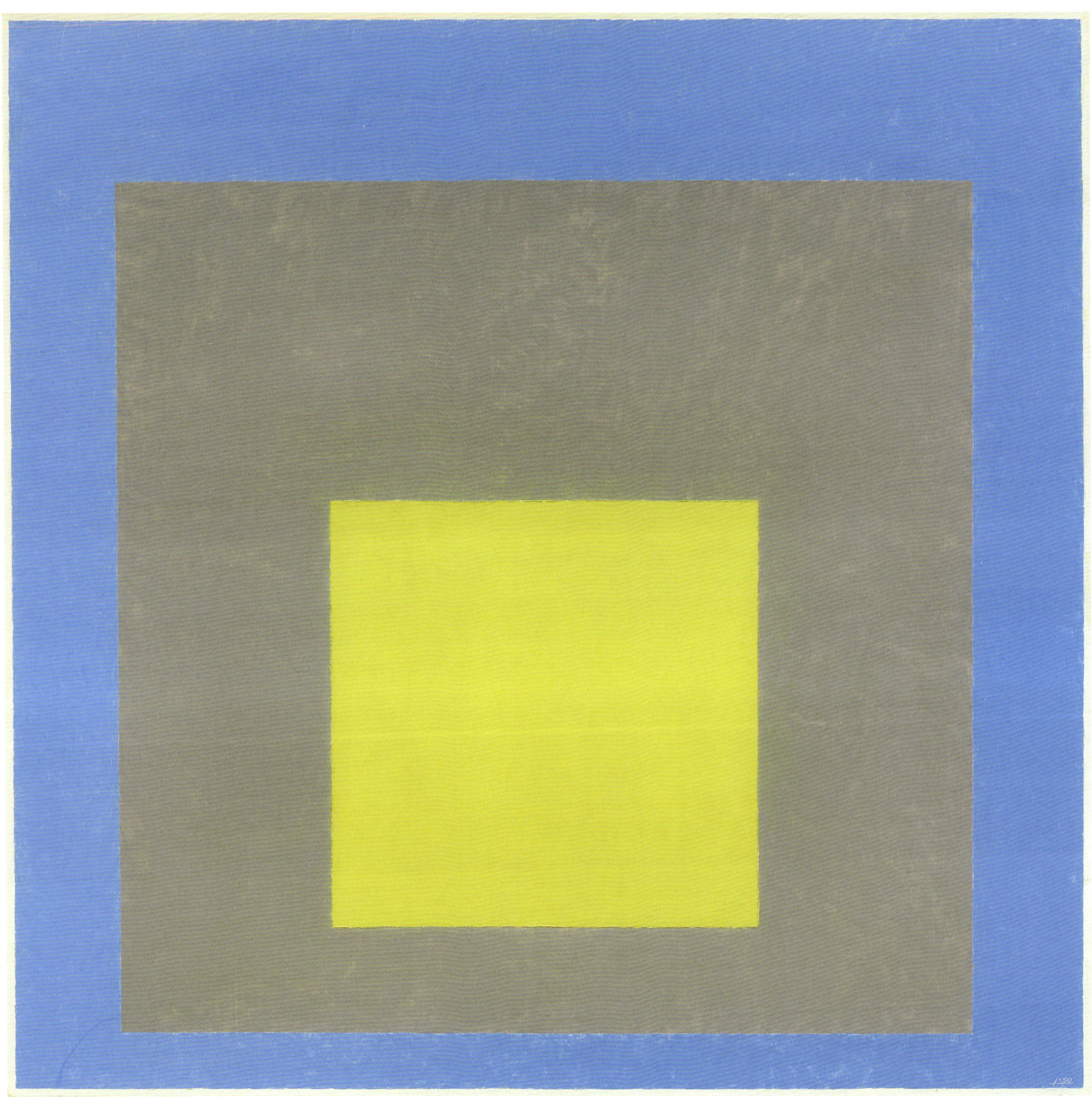

CONTENTS

PLATES

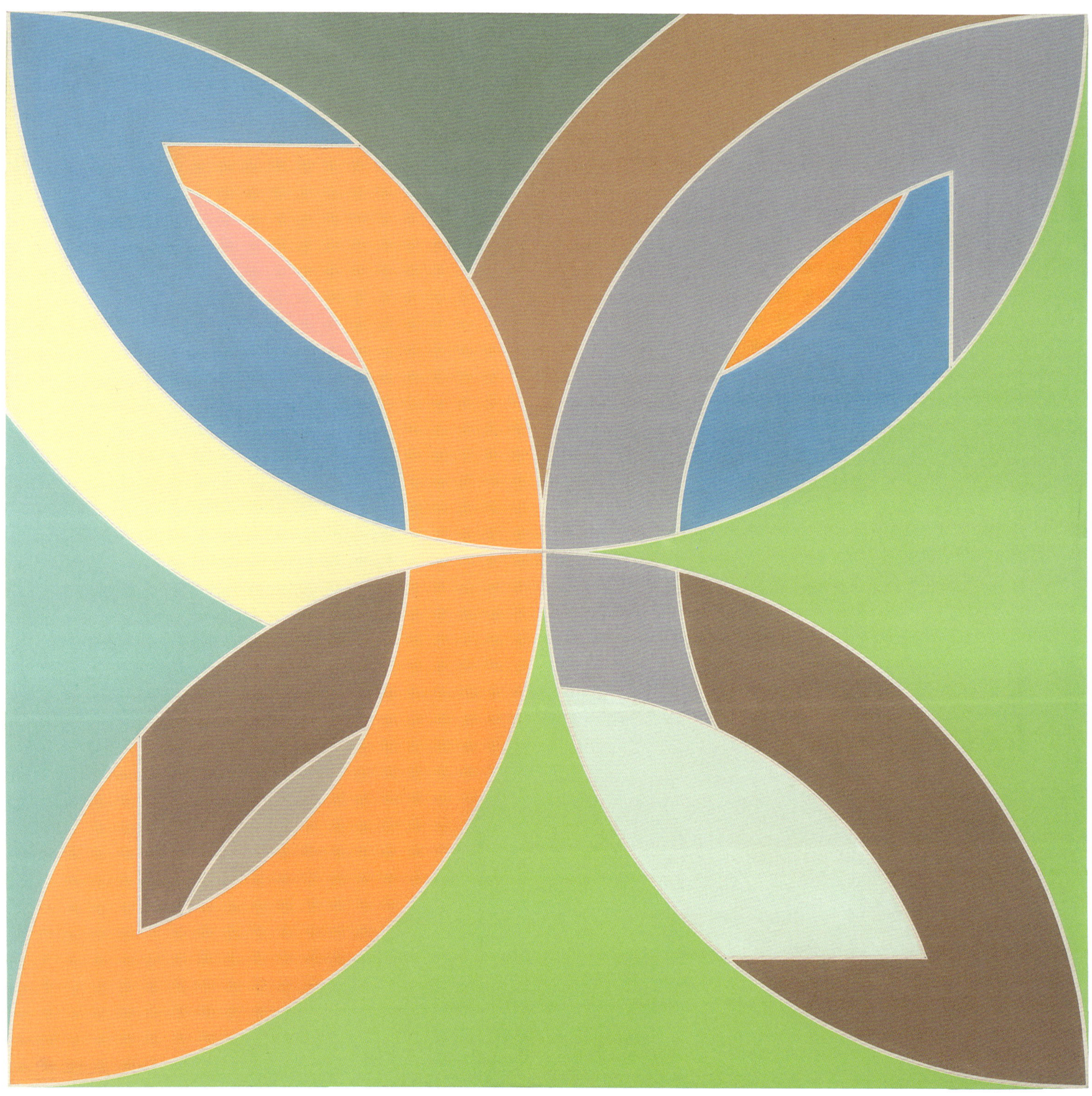

DIRECTOR'S FOREWORD
NATIONAL GALLERY OF ART, WASHINGTON

Starting in 1958, Robert and Jane Meyerhoff devoted themselves to collecting art. It was more than a hobby, it was a passion—the omnipresent focus of their lives together. They gathered more than three hundred works by fifty artists, collecting avidly until 2004, when Jane passed away. In this alone, there is nothing very unusual. What makes the Meyerhoffs' story remarkable is the sharply focused nature of their collecting, the astonishing quality of the art they acquired, and their decision, in mid-career, to give it all away.

The Meyerhoffs' agreement with the National Gallery of Art, which was concluded in 1987, ensured that the collection would remain free and open to the public in perpetuity. With this gift, they joined a small group of patrons whose generosity has been instrumental to the establishment and growth of the nation's collection. Understandably, the Meyerhoffs wanted to continue to live with the art that meant so much to them, so the gift was a promise. But it was also more than a promise. Starting in 1989, with the donation of Clyfford Still's majestic painting *1951–N* (pl. 44), they began to part with their works, one after another. (Before that, in 1986, they had donated Barnett Newman's cycle of fifteen paintings, *The Stations of the Cross: Lema Sabachthani* [pls. 1–15], but these fall into a somewhat different category, as they came straight to the National Gallery without stopping on the Meyerhoffs' walls.) More than fifty gifts have followed, part of an ongoing philanthropic act of national and historic proportions.

This exhibition features all of the paintings and sculptures already given to the National Gallery, rounded out with six paintings borrowed from Robert Meyerhoff's own galleries. The focus of the collection is obvious at once: American painting of the postwar era, including Abstract Expressionists, such as Grace Hartigan, Hans Hofmann, and Mark Rothko; artists associated with the Pop art movement, such as Roy Lichtenstein and Robert Rauschenberg; such living masters as Jasper Johns, Ellsworth Kelly, Brice Marden, James Rosenquist, and Frank Stella; and relative youngsters, such as Eric Fischl, David Salle, and Terry Winters. There are just enough Europeans—Anthony Caro, Jean Dubuffet, and Howard Hodgkin—to make it impossible to give the collection a nationalist spin. This presentation is not about American art, but about great art that happens to have been made, for the most part, in America.

The reason to focus on the Meyerhoff works already given to the National Gallery was simple. With the East Building galleries closed for renovation and expansion from 2014 through 2016, it would have been a pity to let these works languish in storage. When Richard Benefield, deputy director of the Fine Arts Museums of San Francisco, expressed interest in borrowing the works, I asked Harry Cooper, our curator and head of modern art, to collaborate with him. I am indebted to both of them, to many colleagues at the National Gallery and the Fine Arts Museums, and, above all, to Robert Meyerhoff. This exhibition represents a historic outing for the Meyerhoff Collection, for it is the first time that a significant portion of it has been shown outside of the Baltimore-Washington area. It is fitting that the city of San Francisco, with its strong commitment to modern art, would provide an eager venue for the occasion.

On behalf of Robert Meyerhoff and his late wife, Jane, I invite you to step into one of the greatest collections of modern art ever assembled. If your eyes have been closed to modern art, I believe this may open them; if they are open already, they will widen.

EARL A. POWELL III

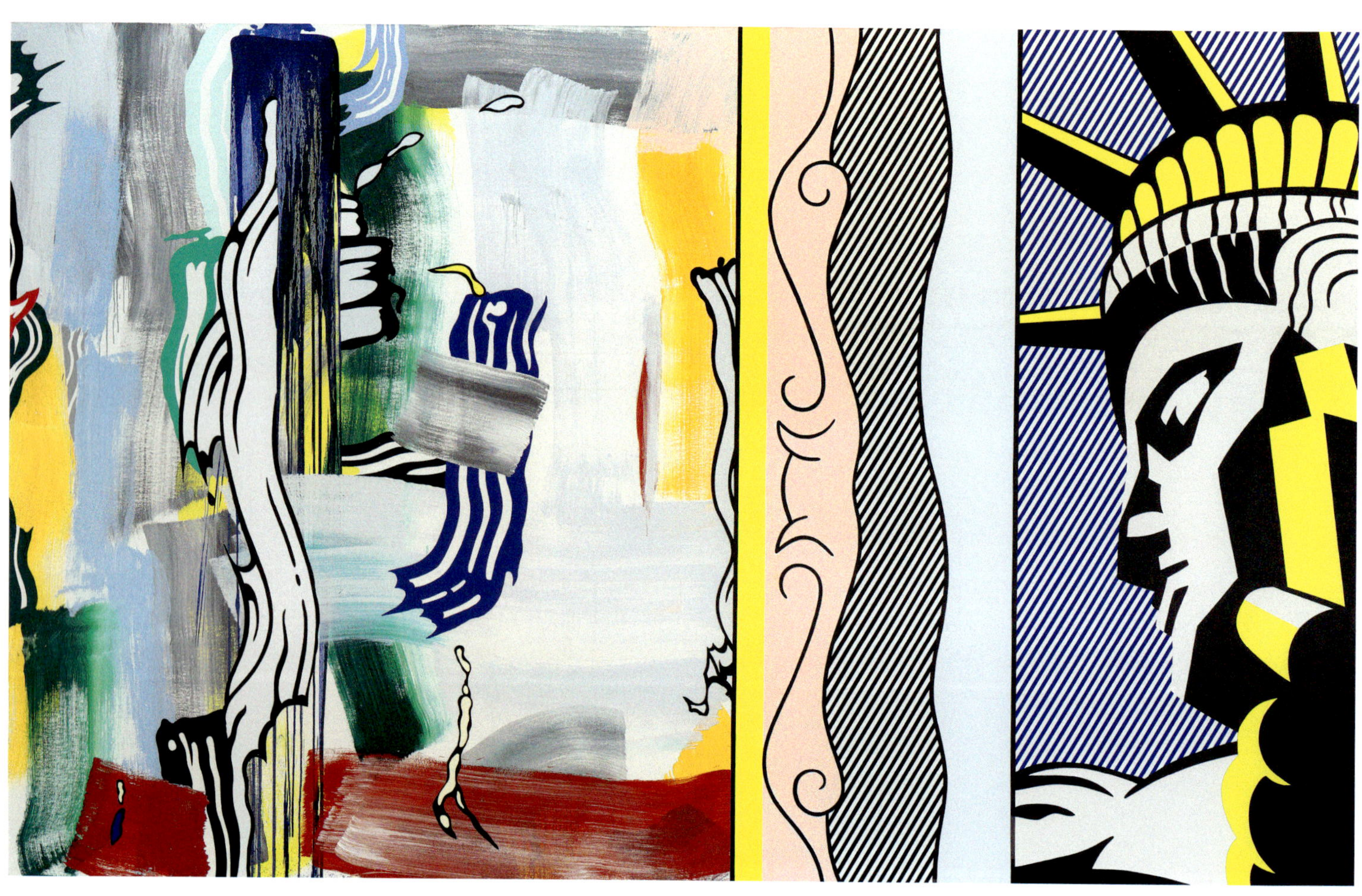

INTRODUCTION

HARRY COOPER

This exhibition marks the first time that a selection of works from the Robert and Jane Meyerhoff Collection, one of the great collections of American painting of the postwar era, has been displayed anywhere outside the Washington-Baltimore area. Thus, it is imperative to offer some background before turning to the works of art themselves.

Jane B. Meyerhoff (1924–2004) and her husband, Robert (b. 1924), always dated the beginning of their collection to the spring of 1958, when they discovered Hans Hofmann's painting *Autumn Gold* (1957; pl. 28). But the story is not that straightforward. They actually began collecting soon after 1947, when Jane's father, Harry A. Bernstein, married the Baltimore artist Ruth Kuff. Ruth inspired Harry to become interested in art and start collecting; Jane and Robert, who had themselves gotten married just two years earlier, in turn "contracted the disease" (in Jane's words) and gradually found themselves traveling to museums and galleries all over the world.[1] Their travels were interrupted in 1955 when Jane contracted polio. During her convalescence, she enrolled in a correspondence course in art appreciation taught by Bates Lowry, a noted art historian then teaching at the University of California, Riverside. "Mr. Lowry helped me to *see* while I was looking," Jane recalled.[2] When her father died in 1957, she decided to work with the director of the Baltimore Museum of Art, Adelyn Breeskin, to establish a memorial collection there in his name.

Asked many years later about the Hofmann acquisition, Jane explained:

> I had been looking with Mrs. Breeskin to make selections for a collection to honor my father at the Baltimore Museum. We all loved Hofmann's *Autumn Gold*, but it would have taken half the memorial money. I took Bob back to see it later. He decided to have his [real estate] company buy it. The Hofmann was borrowed for the [1960] Venice Biennale and was mistakenly returned not to Bob's office but to our house. We hung it, forcing out a lot of other things we had. Bob was prescient and bought the painting from his firm five years later. He had decided he wanted to own it himself. Hofmann was about the only modern artist Bob had seen at this time, and I didn't know much more myself.[3]

And so, through a combination of instinct, vicissitude, and tenacity, a collection began, with Jane as the driving force and Robert as an increasingly equal partner.

Impressed by Jane's eye, Breeskin had encouraged her to start collecting for herself, not just for her father's memorial collection. Formative experiences quickly followed. The Meyerhoffs saw *The New American Painting* at the Museum of Modern Art in New York in 1959 after its tour of eight European countries.[4] The exhibition's roster included many artists whose works would end up in their collection: William Baziotes, Philip

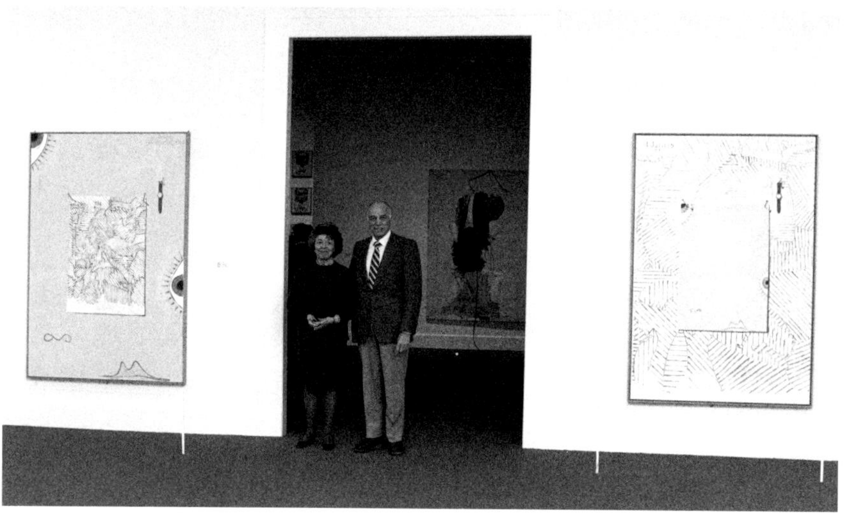

Robert and Jane Meyerhoff at the National Gallery of Art, October 24, 1988

Guston, Grace Hartigan, Franz Kline, Willem de Kooning, Barnett Newman, Jackson Pollock, Mark Rothko, Clyfford Still, and Bradley Walker Tomlin. Soon, for reasons of economics as well as adventure, the Meyerhoffs were drawn to the next generation of American artists. (It was rather late to start collecting Abstract Expressionists, who were well established by then and whose prices were swiftly rising.) They became close to dealers such as Sam Kootz, Sidney Janis, Leo Castelli, Ivan Karp, Ben Heller, and Irving Blum, who were happy to educate the couple and introduce them to many of the younger artists. In 1959, the women's committee of the Baltimore Museum asked Jane to join; in that capacity, she began to visit New York frequently to scout for works for the museum's Sales and Rental Gallery. Once again, she was collecting both for herself and for the Baltimore Museum. For herself, she acquired a painting by her good friend Grace (aka George) Hartigan, one of the few women who was able to hold her own in the macho world of Abstract Expressionist New York. It was the first work by a younger artist to enter the collection. (In addition to the Hofmann painting, previous purchases included works by Baziotes, Tomlin, and Joseph Cornell.) Jane further sharpened her eye by taking a course based on Josef Albers's seminal text, *Interaction of Color* (1963), with a certified instructor in Baltimore. (Robert enrolled as well but did not have the time to stick with it.)

A second formative museum-going experience for the Meyerhoffs came in early 1960 when they saw *Sixteen Americans*, also at the Museum of Modern Art. The exhibition introduced a young Frank Stella with his redoubtable Black paintings and also included rooms devoted to Jasper Johns, Ellsworth Kelly, and Robert Rauschenberg; these four artists would become the core of the Meyerhoffs' collection. Their enthusiasm for Rauschenberg was especially precocious: they had first discovered him at the 1959 Carnegie International in Pittsburgh and tried to buy *Painting with Red Letter S* (1957) from that exhibition, only to find that the Albright-Knox Art Gallery had beaten them to the punch. They soon compensated for this by acquiring an important transfer drawing as well as the painting *Archive* (1963; pl. 35). Both Robert and Jane developed a lasting friendship with Rauschenberg after he visited Baltimore in 1964 as lighting director for Merce Cunningham's dance company. On the other hand, the Meyerhoffs began to collect Stella, Kelly, and Johns only in the 1970s, once they had moved from Baltimore to Fitzhugh Farm, north of the city, and had more room for art. The years between 1977 and 1989 were ones of phenomenal growth for the collection (aided from 1981 on by spectacular yet simple new galleries built onto their home). Two more artists were added to the core group, one from the same generation, Roy Lichtenstein, and one from the next generation, Brice Marden. Close friendships grew with these artists as well. The Meyerhoffs' collecting was finally brought to a close, more than fifty years after it had started, with Jane's passing in 2004. By then the Meyerhoffs had established one of the world's major

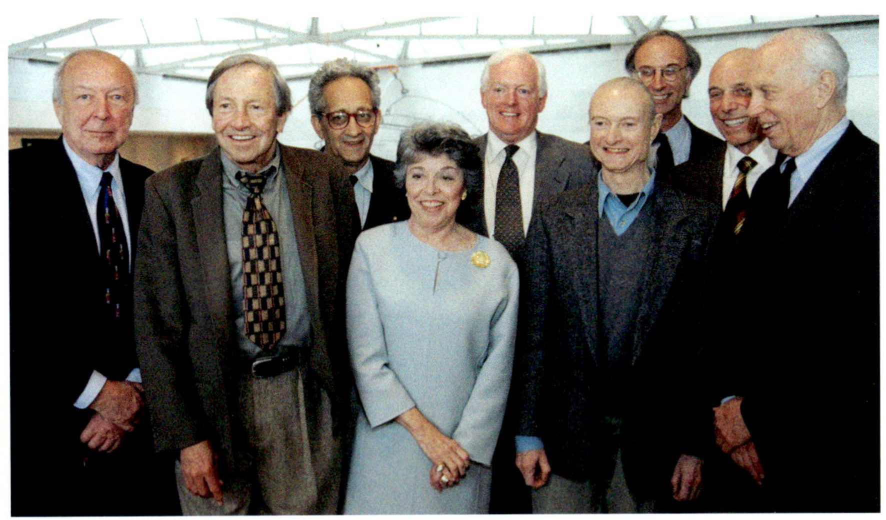

Jasper Johns, Robert Rauschenberg, Frank Stella, Jane Meyerhoff, Earl A. Powell III, Roy Lichtenstein, Mark Rosenthal, Robert Meyerhoff, and Ellsworth Kelly at the press event for the National Gallery of Art exhibition *The Robert and Jane Meyerhoff Collection: 1945–1995*, March 29, 1996

collections of modern art, with more than three hundred works by fifty artists in various media.

Equally important background to this exhibition concerns the relationship between the Meyerhoffs and the National Gallery of Art. It began, at least on a personal level, with a visit to Fitzhugh Farm from Jack Cowart, then the museum's curator of twentieth-century art, in 1984. A meeting with the gallery's director, J. Carter Brown, followed the next year. By 1987, it was agreed that the Meyerhoff Collection would be donated to the National Gallery after the Meyerhoffs' passing and that the museum would operate Fitzhugh Farm as an exhibition and study center, beginning with a five-year trial period. While these negotiations were underway, the Meyerhoffs donated funds for the purchase of Barnett Newman's most ambitious work, *The Stations of the Cross: Lema Sabachthani*, a cycle of fifteen paintings made between 1958 and 1966. (They understood the importance of the *Stations*, having seen them at the Solomon R. Guggenheim Museum, New York, in 1966 and at the inaugural exhibition of the East Building of the National Gallery in 1978—the only two times they had been shown publicly.) These extraordinary acts of generosity will define the Gallery's collection of modern art for future generations, and have already had their effect: some fifty works have been donated outright and displayed. Indeed, these works, supplemented with six lent by Robert from Fitzhugh Farm, are the focus of this exhibition.

In the years since the 1987 agreement, the National Gallery has presented the collection twice, in 1996 and 2009. These were two very different exhibitions: the first, curated by Mark Rosenthal with considerable input from Jane Meyerhoff, presented the works much as they were displayed at Fitzhugh Farm, with individual rooms devoted to the six core artists flanked, as it were, by galleries devoted to the Abstract Expressionists and the younger artists. (Mark asked me to write two entries for the catalogue—my first publication in art history.) The opening was an affair to remember, with all of the Meyerhoff artists and much of the art world in attendance, including such aging legends as Leo Castelli and Philip Johnson. The second exhibition, which I curated, was smaller in size and different in organization. Rather than adhere to a monographic presentation, I shuffled the deck, presenting the works in ten groupings informed by techniques, forms, and themes in the work. (Robert encouraged me in this by recalling that Jane had sometimes thought about a similar reshuffling.) Once again, the opening was a memorable event, saddened only by the absence of Lichtenstein, Rauschenberg, and Jane herself.

The present exhibition is different again by definition: its occasion is the closure of the East Building galleries for renovation and expansion. Our director, Earl A. Powell III, was intent on not letting the paintings and sculptures that the Meyerhoffs already had donated to the National Gallery over the years lie in storage for the duration of the work. Richard Benefield, deputy director of the Fine Arts Museums of San Francisco, expressed strong interest in exhibiting these works. A particular challenge in assembling the exhibition was the fact that the existing donations had been made over a number of years and for a variety of reasons. In some cases (e.g., Eric Fischl's *Saigon, Minnesota*), the Meyerhoffs donated works that were too large to fit easily into their own galleries; in other cases (e.g., Agnes Martin's *Untitled #2*), they had lent a work to a National Gallery exhibition and decided to leave it there rather than retrieve it. On the other hand, deliberate decisions were made to gift some of the key works of the collection, including paintings by Hofmann, Johns, Ad Reinhardt, Stella, and Still. Due to the somewhat arbitrary nature of the gifts, three of the core Meyerhoff artists were not included: Kelly, Rauschenberg, and Marden. However, thanks to Robert's unflagging generosity, we have been able to supplement the exhibition with works by these three artists and with paintings by Guston, Rothko, and Terry Winters that I regard as crucial to any Meyerhoff exhibition.

Another way that the present exhibition differs from the past ones concerns this catalogue. The 1996 catalogue included one essay for each artist, and the 2009 catalogue included one essay for each category or theme. This time I decided to dedicate a single brief essay to each work in the exhibition (or, in a few cases, to multiple works by the same artist); my colleagues in the Department of Modern Art, Molly Donovan, James Meyer, Jennifer Roberts, Kerry Rose, and Paige Rozanski, wrote these. I have contributed a longer essay on *The Stations of the Cross* and an overview of the exhibition that suggests to the viewer a variety of pathways through it.

Working on this, the second (or even third) Meyerhoff exhibition of my career, has been a pleasure, a privilege, and a continuing education. As I have come to know the collection better, thanks in large part to the time I have spent looking at it with Robert, I have come to know my own tastes and instincts better as well, and to develop, I think, at least something of what Jane liked to call a "thinking eye."

---

1 Jane Meyerhoff, "The Collector's Perspective," in *The Robert and Jane Meyerhoff Collection: 1958–1979*, ed. Nina C. Sundell (Baltimore: Baltimore Museum of Art, 1980), n.p.

2 Ibid.

3 Jane Meyerhoff to Jack Cowart, then curator of twentieth-century art at the National Gallery of Art, from an unpublished typescript of conversations that also included Robert Meyerhoff, 1991–1993, 4–5.

4 Ibid., 26.

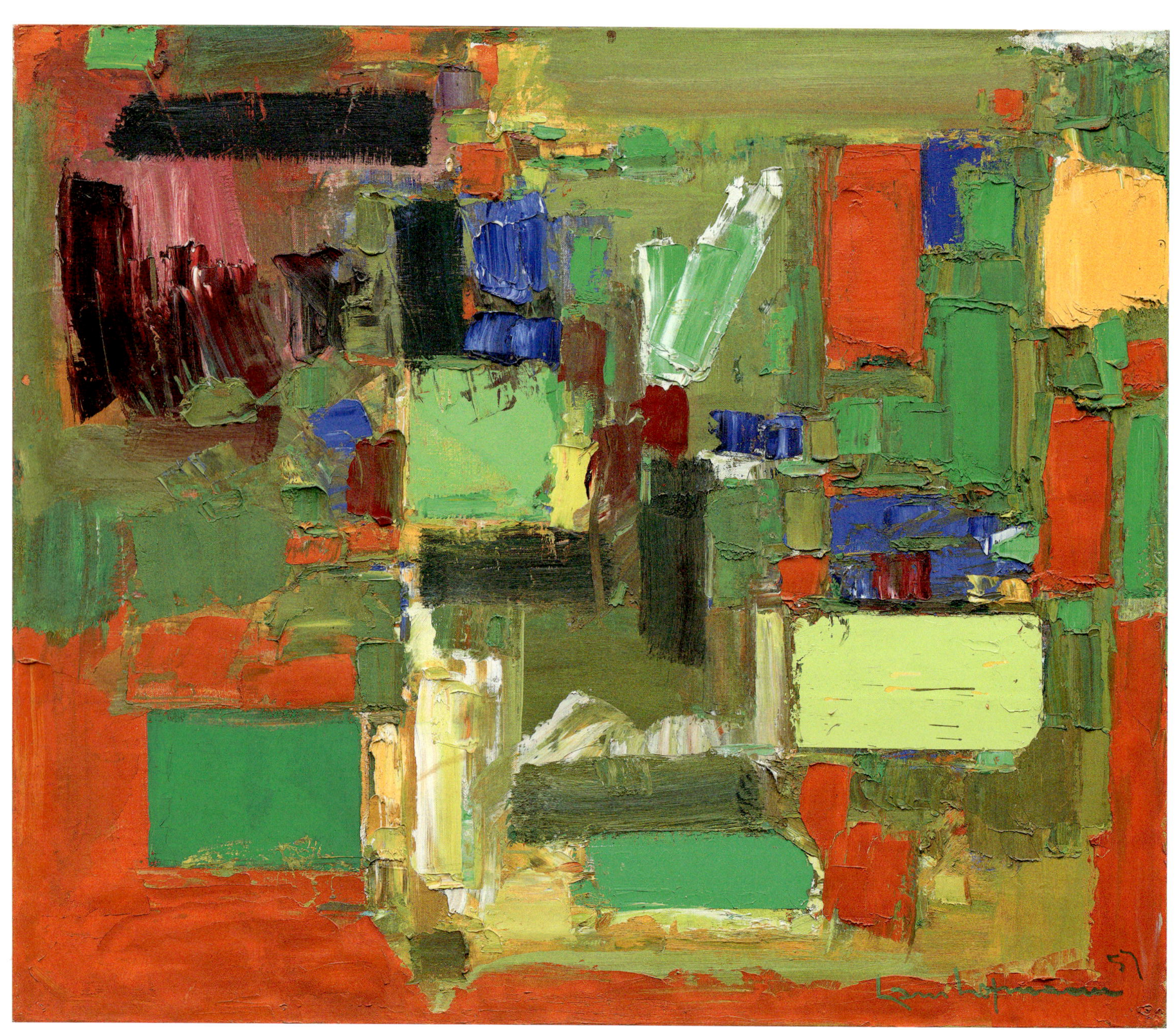

HOFMANN'S HINTS
A JOURNEY THROUGH THE MEYERHOFF COLLECTION

HARRY COOPER

This painting taught us to see how the manipulation of color can energize a two-dimensional surface.[1]

So wrote Jane Meyerhoff about Hans Hofmann's *Autumn Gold* (1957; pl. 28), the painting that inaugurated the Meyerhoff Collection, which she and her husband, Robert, built over more than five decades. The statement could not be simpler, but it speaks volumes. Indeed, it forms a kind of golden rule for the collection. Rabbi Hillel reportedly said of the actual Golden Rule, "That is the whole Torah; the rest is explanation; go and learn."[2] So, let's go, starting with the statement itself, word by word.

This painting. Despite the inclusion of sculptures and reliefs, the Meyerhoff Collection is essentially one of paintings, initiated in 1958, when painting was on top of the world, the paragon of the arts. *Taught us to see.* Neither innate nor passive, seeing is a skill that can be developed by cultivating what Paul Klee—as Jane Meyerhoff liked to note—called the thinking eye.[3] *How the manipulation.* From the Latin *manipulus*, meaning "handful," manipulation connotes not just arrangement or distribution, but also the manual act and the traces it leaves on the surface. *Of color.* The climax of the sentence, color is the object of study, the keynote of the collection. *Can energize.* This puts us firmly at mid-century, when Jackson Pollock spoke of painting as "energy and motion made visible," or as "energy, motion, and the other inner forces."[4] *A two-dimensional surface.* Here is another mid-century idea, championed by the critic Clement Greenberg, who asserted in 1962 that the essence of painting was "flatness and the delimitation of flatness."[5] But it is also an idea with a long history, going back at least to the painter Maurice Denis, who declared in 1890 that "a picture, before being a battle horse, a nude, an anecdote or whatnot, is essentially a flat surface covered with colors assembled in a certain order"[6] (see fig. 1). Even in a figurative painting, abstract considerations take priority, not necessarily in sequence but always in importance: this is the credo of what is sometimes called formalism.

Hofmann's *Autumn Gold*, the subject of Jane Meyerhoff's statement, not only was the first painting to enter the collection; it also stands at the head of two broad pathways through it, which I will call Color/Light and Plot/Structure. Before heading down each one, let us explore the painting itself.

AUTUMN GOLD

For Hofmann, who taught art in Germany from 1915 to 1932 and in the United States from 1934 to 1958, the great animator of painting was tension. He believed that traditional ways of achieving spatial illusion were "sterile," but he also thought that reacting against them with a niggling obedience to the flatness of the canvas was "passive." The way out of this dilemma was to create an equivalent of spatial experience by using explicitly two-dimensional means—slabs of color, frank brushstrokes, evident texture—arranged in high mutual tension, a state that Hofmann famously dubbed "push and pull."[7]

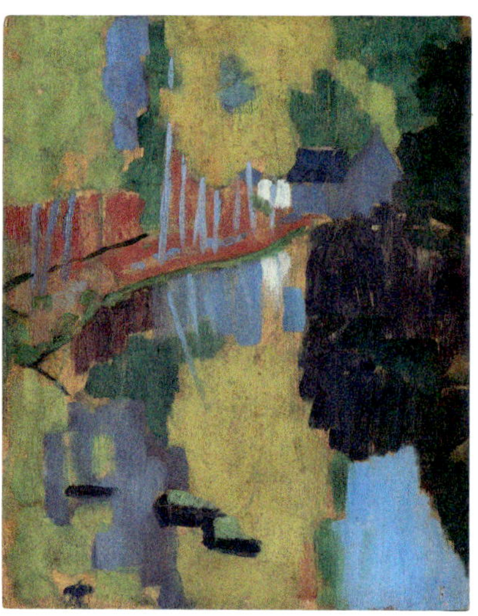

Fig. 1: Paul Sérusier, *The Talisman*, 1888. Oil on wood, 10 5/8 x 8 1/4 in. (27 x 21 cm). Musée d'Orsay, Paris

The dynamics of Hofmann's system are on full, almost didactic display in *Autumn Gold*, painted just as he was retiring from teaching to focus on his art. The most striking tension in the painting is between red and green, complementary colors occupying opposite places on the color wheel. (The complement of any given primary pigment, whether blue, red, or yellow, is the hue produced by mixing the other two primaries.) Nineteenth-century color theorists such as Michel Eugène Chevreul formulated the perceptual effects of complementary colors, observing that when any two colors are juxtaposed, the apparent color of each shifts toward the complement of the other. In the special case where two adjacent colors are complements, each will be perceived more intensely as itself—the red more red, the green more green. Georges Seurat had applied this lesson one way, juxtaposing small points of complementary color to achieve what he hoped would be the vivid optical mixture of a third color (fig. 2); Hofmann applied the lesson very differently in *Autumn Gold*, pairing large slabs of red and green in order to intensify the viewer's experience of each.[8] The fact that the two colors are of the same value (they would be hard to distinguish in a black-and-white reproduction) heightens the contest, setting up an optical buzz between them.

Hofmann also understood that warmer colors tend to advance toward the observer, while cooler colors recede. At lower left, he works against this effect, surrounding the recessive green with a background of red, which forces the green forward as figure (even while a thick stroke of red overlapping the top of the green rectangle keeps it pinned down) (fig. 3). He does the opposite, less programmatically, at upper right, where a vertical slab of red is surrounded by greens as well as by a note of blue. This is push and pull at its most complex, with warm and cool colors advancing and receding in tension with the suggestions of figure and ground.

We get some relief from this red-green drama in the form of subsidiary color relationships that also involve complements. Blue is often accompanied by orange. A brushy violet at upper left faces off against a tile of yellow-green at lower right: the passages are opposite in texture and value as well as color. At center, the play of complements is resolved in two thick strokes of a rich brown, one horizontal and the other vertical. They remind the art student in us that the best way to attain a vivid neutral color is to mix complements together.

Another set of tensions involves texture. Once again, Hofmann explores all possible variations on the theme. His palette knife can scrape, smear, or build up, producing flat areas or textured slabs; his brush can drag paint slowly or quickly and leave more or less evident traces of its bristles. Hybridity is his textural signature. Indeed, Hofmann's distinctive trait is his lack of restraint, his unwillingness to say "no" to any color or device in a given canvas. How one feels about his art depends partly on how one feels about this aspect of his personality.

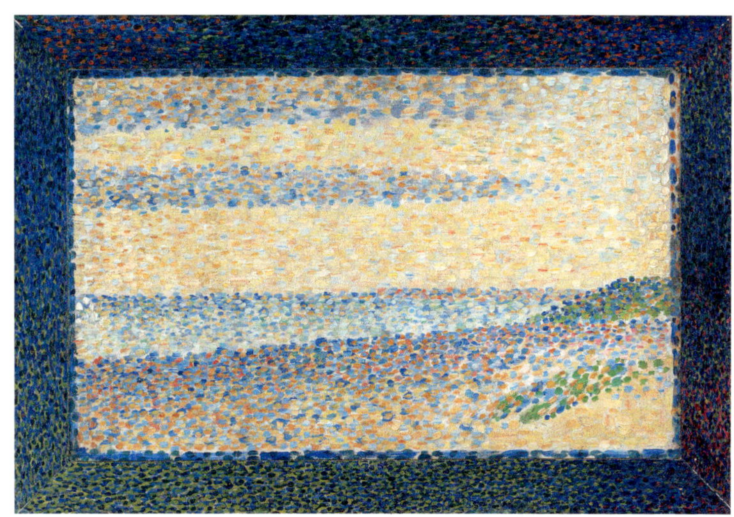

Fig. 2: Georges Seurat, *Seascape (Gravelines)*, 1890. Oil on panel, 8 7/16 x 12 in. (21.5 x 30.5 cm). National Gallery of Art, Washington. Collection of Mr. and Mrs. Paul Mellon

COLOR/LIGHT: ALBERS, DILLER, KELLY

If the acquisition of *Autumn Gold* offered the Meyerhoffs one kind of pedagogy, they sought out another in the 1960s, before their collecting had shifted into high gear, by enrolling in Josef Albers's color course, given in Baltimore by one of his former students. (Albers was retired by then: he had taught at the Bauhaus from 1922 to 1932, Black Mountain College from 1933 to 1949, and Yale University from 1950 to 1958.) In a sense, then, our young couple studied with both Albers and Hofmann, the two most influential art teachers of the time. Fittingly, they are the senior artists of the collection, both born in Germany in the 1880s, one generation before the Abstract Expressionists and two before the postwar painters at the core of the collection. At the risk of oversimplifying, we could say that Hofmann and Albers represent poles of expressiveness and restraint, the maximal and the minimal, Apollo and Dionysus. Jane once remarked that her husband, Robert, inclined toward the former, she toward the latter.[9] Between them, the collection developed.

Let us explore the contrast a little further. Hofmann composed his colored rectangles dramatically, drawing on the principles of dynamic equilibrium and asymmetrical balance he learned from Piet Mondrian and the painters of the De Stijl movement: note how *Autumn Gold* is organized around a main horizontal-vertical intersection below and left of center. Albers chose to limit himself for decades to nested, concentric squares, effectively restricting compositional choice to color alone.[10] (The *Homage to the Square* series occupied him from 1950 until his death.) Albers believed that color was best perceived once subjectivity had been hushed. His paint handling is as restrained as Hofmann's is extravagant. In an era of Action Painting (the name given to Abstract Expressionism by the critic Harold Rosenberg), Albers spoke pointedly about "acting color."[11] According to one of his poems, "To be able to perceive it [art] / we need to be receptive / therefore art is there / where art seizes us."[12] The very passivity that Hofmann decried, Albers embraced.

By keeping composition relatively neutral in the *Homages*, Albers focuses our attention on the "interaction of color," to cite the title of his famous 1963 teaching text, which was the basis of the course the Meyerhoffs took. The *Homages* are autonomous works of art, not pedagogical demonstrations, yet each seems to make a discrete point about color. In *Study for Homage to the Square: Light Rising* (1950, altered 1959; pl. 16), an early member of the series, Albers's goal seems to be to intensify the yellow of the central square. He achieves this by painting the immediate frame of the yellow in a neutral gray, which emphasizes the yellow as a singular color, while painting the outer frame in a cool blue, which sets off the warmth of the yellow while avoiding direct color competition.

The subtitle of the painting, *Light Rising*, inserts a figurative suggestion into an abstract painting. More importantly, the phrase points to light rather than color as

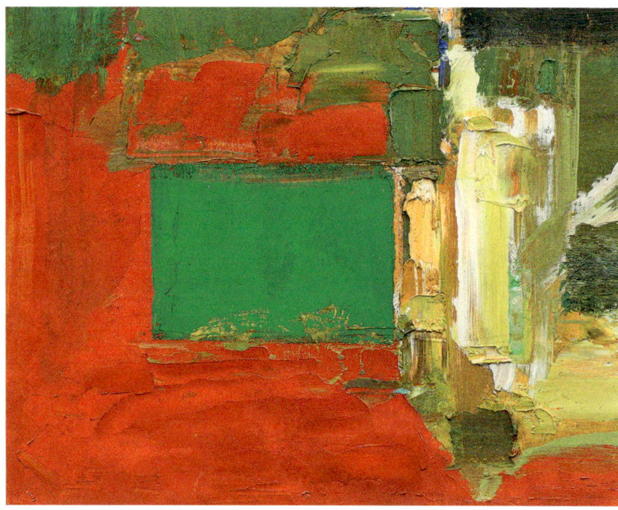

Fig. 3: Hans Hofmann, *Autumn Gold*, 1957. Detail, pl. 28

the subject of the work. (It is not called "Yellow Rising.") Albers once recalled a 1913 landscape by Edvard Munch in which "there was such a terrific glow that you couldn't look into the sun."[13] He hoped to achieve something of that power himself, to convey "direct light, the light which comes from behind the surface . . . a volume, not a surface illusion."[14] Color (from the Old Latin *colos* or "covering") is superficial; light is deep. With flicks of the palette knife, he applies paint so that the white ground shows through, illuminating the painting from within (fig. 4). Conversely, Hofmann reveled in the application of color as a covering, building up what Greenberg called "a fat, heavy, and eloquent surface," or what Michael Fried called "a skin of paint."[15] In spite of that, Hofmann too sought light as his ultimate goal: "In nature, light creates the color. In the picture, color creates the light."[16]

Standing between Hofmann and Albers is Burgoyne Diller. He combines the former's drama with the latter's restraint, but he also stands outside their dichotomy, for much of his work seeks to suspend the very interactions of color that they both cherished. Painted in 1964, *First Theme* (pl. 21) is one of Diller's last works, wrapping up a series that he started in the 1930s. The surface of the painting is flat and uninflected, focusing all attention on shape and color. What might seem at first glance to be a white square and identically shaped bars of blue and yellow turns out to be, on closer inspection, a slightly horizontal rectangle and two bars of different length and width. Indeed, not one dimension or interval in the painting is repeated. This reflects the emphasis given to non-mathematical, intuitive composition by the artists of De Stijl, especially Mondrian, Diller's hero.

Another De Stijl principle, the autonomy of individual colors, is expressed in the separation of the three shapes of *First Theme*. In his classic work, Mondrian generally kept colors to the edge rather than allowing them into the center of the canvas, which was dominated by white and gray rectangles. Theo van Doesburg, Mondrian's colleague in De Stijl, sometimes went further, using a solid black ground to isolate areas of color and suppress their visual interaction (fig. 5). (Unlike a white ground, a black ground discourages the complementary-colored retinal afterimages that we can see after staring intently at a single colored shape.) Following these principles, *First Theme* combines compositional dynamism—the shapes seem to float freely on the square ground, and the yellow even seems to shoot beyond it—with coloristic stability. It attempts, however quixotically, to stabilize our color perception, to establish each colored shape as isolated and autonomous, a monad.

Seen in retrospect, the Meyerhoffs' acquisition of Diller's painting in 1974 prepared the ground for their major investment in the work of a painter of the next generation, Ellsworth Kelly. Among the seven Kelly paintings in the collection, *Orange Green* (pl. 30) from 1966 is the earliest as well as the first one they acquired. Here we find Kelly at a transitional moment, using simpler forms and a larger scale than in his 1950s work, without yet arriving

Fig. 4: Josef Albers, *Study for Homage to the Square: Light Rising,* 1950, altered 1959. Detail, pl. 16

at the device that would define his career: the use of a separate canvas for each monochrome unit of any given composition, which gives each color-shape a separate and equal claim on our attention. In *Orange Green*, separation is clearly achieved by the choice of contrasting colors and the sharp edge between them. Equality is less certain: the orange shape is certainly dominant, appearing as a figure against the green ground, but the fact that the orange occupies a smaller area than the green and is not as saturated gives the green a more active role. Seen this way, the green is not just a container but also a shape (or actually three shapes) in its own right. The orange appears set into the green rather than lying on top of it, further equating the two. *Orange Green* is a picture of monadization in progress and, relatedly, of figure-ground in demolition.

At about 88 by 65 inches, just exceeding average human height and reach, *Orange Green* is the largest work we have encountered so far. Hofmann, Albers, and Diller were easel painters; Kelly, by contrast, inherited the ambitious scale of Abstract Expressionism, of Pollock, Newman, Rothko, and Still. This literally monumental shift was overdetermined by the need to provide space for full-bodied gestures; to create fields that would encompass the viewer; to rival walls and murals in public impact; to create real spaces rather than framed images. But whatever the particular goals of the different Abstract Expressionists, they shared a desire to escape what they saw as the aestheticism of European painting, the balancing of pictorial elements within the rectangle of the canvas. The next generation went farther still. The scale and simplicity of Kelly's elements give them an inevitability: although we know that they have been shaped and placed by the artist, we feel that they are beyond manipulation. This same scale aids Kelly's attack on figure-ground relations, for an image that fills our visual field tends to become all figure or all ground rather than dividing into figure and ground. If we cannot distance the image, we cannot master and organize it according to our normal perceptual habits. The result is an energized surface of equal intensity—one of the touchstones of modernist painting, and a prerequisite for full-fledged abstraction.

Color has a privileged place in this history: there is nothing like a single expanse of color to declare the surface and fill the eye. (It is no surprise that one of Mark Rothko's favorite paintings was Henri Matisse's *The Red Studio*, 1911 [fig. 6].) But in the very act of filling the eye, color may dissolve the surface on which it rests, delivering the beholder into an optical space. This tension between color as matter and color as light, which we have seen already in the contrast between Hofmann and Albers, has been a defining one for as long as people have theorized color and practiced painting. Clyfford Still's *1951–N* (pl. 44) presents us with a towering cliff of thickly knifed red-brown paint relieved only by touches of the primary colors. Painted in 1969, Mark Rothko's *Untitled* (pl. 39), by contrast, offers depth as much as surface: its suggestion of penetrable

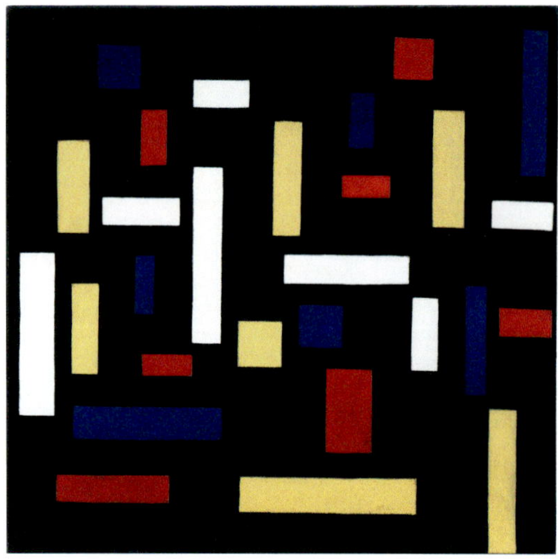

Fig. 5: Theo van Doesburg, *Compositie VII: 'de drie Gratiën' (Composition VII: The Three Graces)*, 1917. Oil on canvas, 33 1/2 x 33 1/2 in. (85.1 x 85.1 cm). Mildred Lane Kemper Art Museum, Washington University in Saint Louis. University purchase, Yeatman Fund, 1947

space is aided by the way its unusually simple division into two parts suggests a horizon dividing earth and sky. Barnett Newman's *The Stations of the Cross* (1958–1966) (pls. 1–15) bypasses color entirely, attempting to translate raw canvas into pure light. This historical background helps us to see Kelly's *Orange Green* for what it is: a flat declaration of color as color, acknowledging both its optical and its material qualities while privileging neither. Coming after the grand claims of the Abstract Expressionists, Kelly approaches color as a nominalist and a pragmatist—"Orange Green" says it all.

PLOT/STRUCTURE: FISCHL, GUSTON, JOHNS

If abstraction seems to dominate the Meyerhoff Collection, look again. Of the six artists best represented in it, three are firmly abstract (Ellsworth Kelly, Brice Marden, Frank Stella) while three rarely painted a work without figurative content (Jasper Johns, Roy Lichtenstein, Robert Rauschenberg). Let us follow the figurative path through the collection, first by returning to Hofmann's *Autumn Gold*, this time not for its formal operations but for its narrative and figurative suggestions.

We have seen how Hofmann's orchestration of various tensions (of color, value, and texture) in *Autumn Gold* sought to create a two-dimensional equivalent of space and depth. But for Hofmann, abstraction also had to offer an equivalent of what he variously and mystically called inner life, life experience, and the real. He went so far as to suggest that a successful painting has "the quality of flesh—it pulsates, it has sensation, it is not flat."[17] Let us take another look at *Autumn Gold*, starting with the title, which opens up the painting's abstraction to more worldly connotations.

The title *Autumn Gold* recalls Robert Frost's poem "Nothing Gold Can Stay," published in his 1923 collection *New Hampshire* (a book that soon became famous for its poem "Stopping by Woods on a Snowy Evening"):

> Nature's first green is gold,
>
> Her hardest hue to hold.
>
> Her early leaf's a flower;
>
> But only so an hour.
>
> Then leaf subsides to leaf.
>
> So Eden sank to grief,
>
> So dawn goes down to day.
>
> Nothing gold can stay.

Frost's narrative conceit is that the gold of spring buds soon yields to the green of summer before returning to bow out in a brief autumnal blaze. This was more obvious in the poem's first version, which ended differently: "In autumn she achieves / A still more golden blaze / But nothing golden stays."[18] This tale of hues takes on a symbolic dimension as the poem proceeds, equating (in one of Frost's favorite puns) the season of fall with

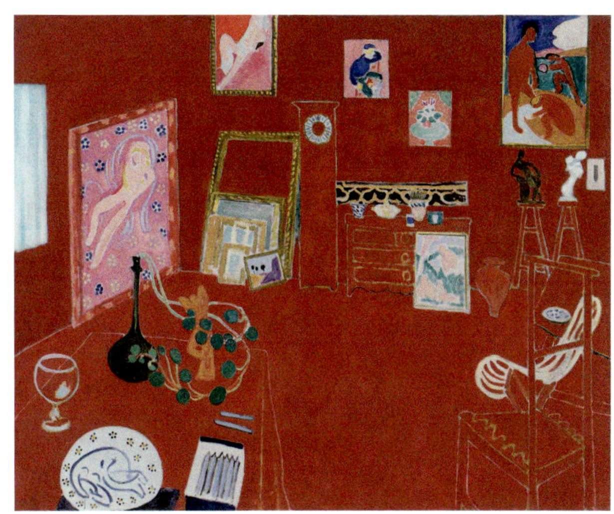

Fig. 6: Henri Matisse, *The Red Studio*, 1911. Oil on canvas, 71 1/4 x 86 1/4 in. (181 x 219.1 cm). The Museum of Modern Art, New York, Mrs. Simon Guggenheim Fund

the Fall of humanity—with original sin and resulting mortality. Thus the poem moves from the green of life and the Garden to the scorched colors of the Fall, with gold making precious but fugitive (and unredemptive) appearances at beginning and end.

It would be a great stretch as well as a travesty of Hofmann's ideas to propose that the painting illustrates the poem. We cannot even be sure that he read it, yet he seems to have had a very similar story in mind. The gold of *Autumn Gold* definitively appears only once on the canvas, in a ravishing patch at the upper right edge, as if poised to depart the scene; it has been nearly pushed out of the picture by the principal drama of green and red, leaving behind only interstitial hints of yellow. This is the coloristic plot of the painting, and it gets encapsulated along the upper edge, where a thick band of green mixed with some red (the longest single stroke in the work) has been dragged over a still-wet stroke of gold, muddying and obscuring it. Nothing gold can stay.

Such a reading goes against the grain of formalism. It is heretical, and the heresy strikes home: Greenberg acknowledged Hofmann's lectures in 1938–1939 as his most important formative influence.[19] And yet, as we know from *Alpine Air* (1962), another Hofmann painting in the collection, the artist was inspired by landscape and often allowed its suggestions into his works and their titles (fig. 7). The question is how far we should let such suggestions color our viewing. Maurice Denis proclaimed that a painting is a flat surface covered with colors *before* it is an anecdote, not *instead* of being one. Could *Autumn Gold* be an anecdote or a story, too? While it is indeed tempting to look at the painting through another lens, perhaps we should respect Jane Meyerhoff's insistence that Hofmann's lesson to her was entirely formal, that nothing narrative can stay.

It would be hard to imagine a painting more different from *Autumn Gold* than Eric Fischl's *Saigon, Minnesota* (1985) (pl. 23). The most traditionally figurative and narrative painting in the collection, it presents eleven human figures and one dog in a unified outdoor setting. Depth is conveyed by a consistent perspective, and the figures are convincing in their anatomy and movement. The strong light is fitting for a scene of summer recreation involving sunbathing, lounging, games, and music. The colors are realistic: the green of the ping-pong table, the brown and white of the dog.

Despite the many obvious dissimilarities between Fischl's painting and *Autumn Gold*, the two works use the same spatio-narrative devices. One of these might be called "action at a distance," to borrow a term from physics. (It refers to the fact that objects can act upon each other at some remove, via electric, magnetic, or gravitational fields, rather than just via actual contact and collision.) Just as the brushy passages of violet and green in *Autumn Gold* call to each other from edge to center, so the central figure in *Saigon, Minnesota*, the boy in the black bathing suit, faces off against a dog streaking toward him from the right edge. This is the climax of the painting, a moment of high tension and frozen movement in an otherwise relaxed, ambling

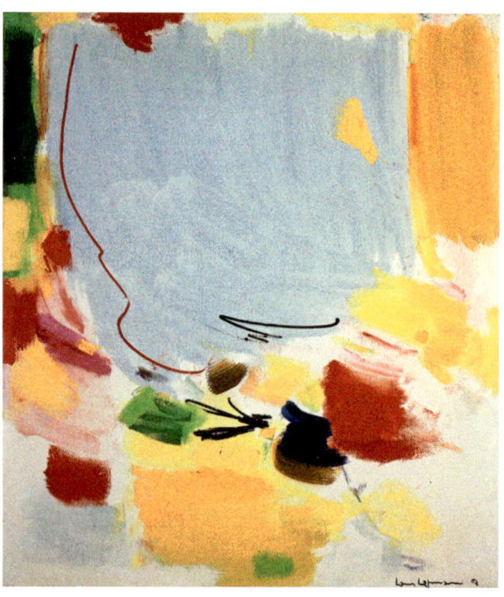

Fig. 7: Hans Hofmann, *Alpine Air*, 1962. Oil on canvas, 23 5/8 x 20 1/2 in. (60 x 52 cm). Collection of Robert and Jane Meyerhoff

scene. (The way that the vertical white line between the sliding glass doors of the house descends to touch the top of the boy's black hair establishes his centrality, fixing our attention on him.) Just as Hofmann's painting has its subplots—the byplay between the green rectangle surrounded by red in one corner and the red rectangle surrounded by green in another—so Fischl's painting has its subsidiary dramas-at-a-distance. The little girl with long black hair interacting with a squatting nude adult male at upper right seems connected to a similar pair at lower left; the green ping-pong table at upper left answers the red air mattress at lower right.

An equal and opposite spatio-narrative device is that of juxtaposition. If Hofmann's painting is an essay on the various ways that any two colored rectangles can touch, and what happens when they do, the action of Fischl's painting is carried primarily by linked *pairs* of figures—not just the two couples already mentioned, but two even more closely joined pairs at the center: the two women who stroll forward, tightly clasped, and the two boys who pose back to back, like conjoined twins who share an arm and leg. Other figures touch on the surface but are separated in illusionistic depth: the four people in the right-hand panel are all "connected" in this way. Likewise, in one of several disturbingly sexual moments, the head of the boy in the white bathing suit is planted firmly in the colored bathing suit of the one-armed man several yards behind him. This paradoxical device, mixing touching with separation, is uniquely available to paintings that present a clear illusion of space. Or is it? In Hofmann's push and pull, a red rectangle may appear firmly soldered to a blue one at one moment of viewing and loom forward in the next. The difference is that in a painting like Fischl's, we are aware of the separation first and the touching second; in Hofmann's, just the opposite is true.

Philip Guston's *Courtroom* of 1970 (pl. 25) presents another multi-figure narrative. As in Fischl's tableau, the narrative is both obscure and disturbing, but now the principal register is that of violence, not sex. The story is an allegory of the painter-as-criminal, perhaps with particular reference to Guston's then-recent abandonment of abstraction for a cartoony figuration. Once again, the principal dramatic device is that of action at a distance, linking center and periphery: a black-sleeved, red-gloved arm extends from the right edge toward the head of a Klansman at center. The space between the pointing finger and the "hood" (to use Guston's own term for that character) is central and charged, a gap across which the spark of the painting's main action travels: *j'accuse*. In the background, white and black rectangles suggesting primed canvases or tacked-up sheets of paper float on a wall, attracting and repelling one another.

The remainder of the narrative is carried by juxtaposition: the hood is jammed up against a trash can full of sticks of wood, used stretcher bars, and a pair of upside-down legs. This pileup is an island, independent of the other elements of the picture; the left-hand shoe just avoids touching one

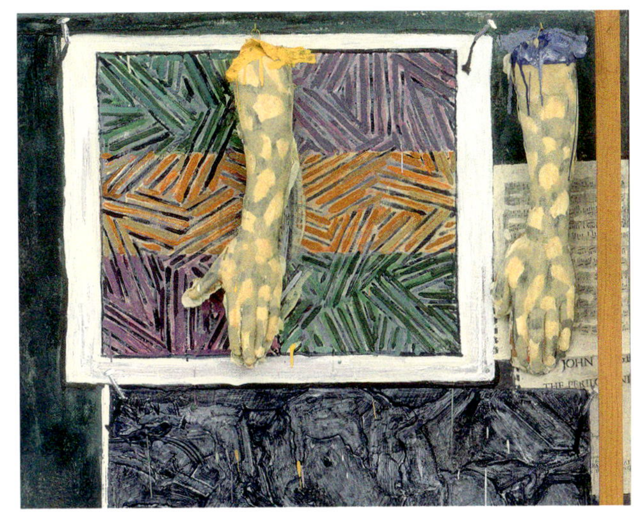

Fig. 8: Jasper Johns, *Perilous Night*, 1982. Detail, pl. 29

of the rectangles on the wall. By keeping these two spatio-narrative devices (action at a distance and juxtaposition) separate, Guston demonstrates them clearly.

Jasper Johns's *Perilous Night* (pl. 29) of 1982 is a less obvious potboiler than Guston's painting, but one that is equally self-referential, presenting a kind of studio scene full of allusions to art history as well as the artist's own biography. Art-historical references abound, including Pablo Picasso's *Weeping Woman* (1937), Matthias Grünewald's *Isenheim Altarpiece* (1512–1516), Cubist trompe l'oeil devices, and Johns's own work. The primary biographical reference is to Johns's friend and collaborator, the composer John Cage, whose composition *The Perilous Night* is not only named in the title, but also carefully represented by a page of sheet music at right.

At the risk of belaboring the point, the most dramatic element of the painting partakes of action at a distance: three cast arms at upper right, spaced evenly along the "wall" of the canvas. They are linked across the gaps not just visually but causally, having been cast from the same subject, the son of a friend of the artist, at three-year intervals. Another case of action at a distance is the two tracings of the Roman soldiers from the Resurrection panel of the altarpiece: they are separated (one occupies the entire left half of the painting, while the other, smaller and rotated, is confined to a rectangle at right), yet, like the cast arms, they are causally and visually linked. The remainder of the painting is structured by tight juxtapositions of rectangles, unremitting and airless. One kind of tracery (Cubist wood graining) is jammed up against another (Grünewald's contours), one system of notation (Cage's musical score) against another (Johns's hatched patterns) (fig. 8). Johns forces visual rhymes together across gaps of history and authorship, culture and intention.

CONCLUSION: ODE TO THE RECTANGLE

I conclude here with a confession. During this journey, I have been trying to complete, or perhaps undo, Maurice Denis's rule: if every painting is a flat surface before it is an anecdote, then—I would add—every painting is also an anecdote before it is a flat surface. My suggestion that paintings as different as Hofmann's *Autumn Gold* and Fischl's *Saigon, Minnesota* may have narratives, and that their narratives rely on similar spatial devices, has, I hope, been persuasive or at least provocative. But there is something more obvious that these two works have in common, something that provides a glue for almost the entire collection, holding it together across the abstract-figurative divide.

If the common goal of the paintings in the collection, and of modernist painting in general, is to energize a two-dimensional surface (recalling Jane Meyerhoff's words), then that surface, whatever else is done to it, must be declared and not denied, respected and not ignored. One sure way to do it, given that the surface is conventionally rectangular, is to paint rectangles within it. No diagonals or

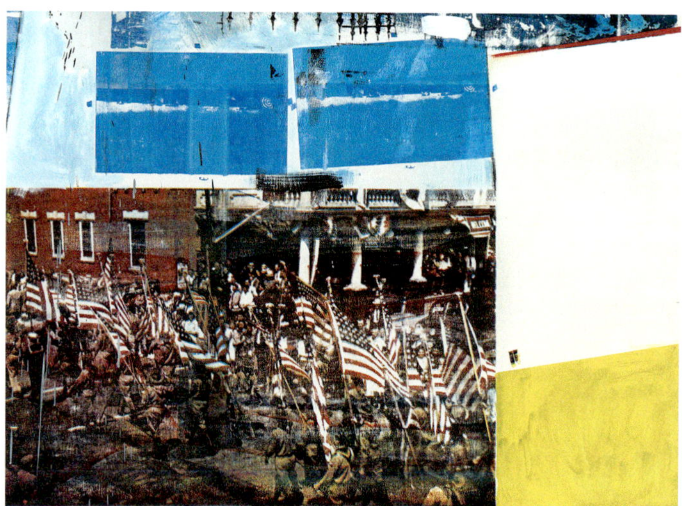

Fig. 9: Robert Rauschenberg, *Archive*, 1963. Detail, pl. 35

curves, no lines of flight, but a studio wall (Johns, Guston), a summer-house facade (Fischl), a "wall" of black (Diller) or green (Kelly)—all rectangles.

Let us take a last look at Fischl's painting. Its illusion of space is sandwiched between two kinds of rectangles: the four panels on which the scene is painted, and the depicted rectangles that bring up the rear of the scene, representing the walls and windows of a house that is parallel to the picture plane.[20] Even the inside of this sandwich is studded with rectangles—a ping-pong table, two air mattresses, a radio, a chair—all seen in perspective, at different angles and depths in the scene, but all rectangular. The most prominent of these rectangles are the canvas panels themselves: because they combine to lend the whole work an unconventional shape, we cannot ignore or forget them. Fischl's painting, unlike simply rectangular ones, is markedly *shaped* (although not as radically shaped as Frank Stella's *Chodorow II* [pl. 42], for example), and this shaping insists, so to speak, that the scene is a construct, an abstraction, a rearrangement of reality. The boys playing ping-pong should be at their table, but it seems to have been kidnapped by the panel at left.[21] Light sources and shadows are mutually contradictory. The deck of reality has been shuffled.

This is not the only painting in the exhibition composed of multiple rectangular supports: the Hodgkin is painted on two tightly joined wood panels, the Marden on two canvas panels, the Salle on four canvas panels, and the Dubuffet on multiple pieces of paper mounted on a single canvas. Even Newman's *The Stations of the Cross: Lema Sabachthani* is arguably a single, multi-panel work, with spaces between the panels. Other works that might also appear to be compound constructions are in fact painted on a continuous canvas: the Johns, both Lichtensteins, and the Rothko.

The most elaborate use of the rectangle in the Meyerhoff Collection may well be Robert Rauschenberg's *Archive* (1963; pl. 35). The various photographic images screened onto the canvas have been arranged in a fairly orderly rectangular grid. (The reliance on an underlying grid to structure a multitude of images would become one of the artist's signatures.) If this is not obvious at once, it is only because the images are bristling with so much activity: wrought iron fence posts, instrument panels, flags, marchers, umbrellas. Here we seem to have come full circle: if *Autumn Gold* is a painting of abstract rectangles encoding a narrative about nature in some way, *Archive* seems to be a painting of rectangular photographic images without a narrative at all. An "archive," after all, is a collection without any necessary order, a place where records are kept, a neutral grid. As Rosalind Krauss has argued, the grid, that master-figure of abstract painting, is hostile to narrative, offering a spatial array rather than a sequence.[22] One can find themes in *Archive* (patriotism, militarism, recreation), and perhaps associated emotional states, but no logic or story.

Even so, Robert Meyerhoff likes to narrate the painting. When friends ask him to tell them what it means, he is happy to oblige. The subject of the painting is the Space Race, he says, which was at its peak in 1963. The red ball at the center represents a blastoff—perhaps Gordon Cooper's earth-orbiting flight of May 1963. The instruments at right are his controls; the helicopters at left will retrieve him from the ocean. The parade of Boy Scouts at the bottom refers to the seven original Mercury astronauts, six of whom, it happens, were Boy Scouts while one was a Sea Scout. (Here Robert points to the one marcher dressed like a sailor.) If his friends are unsatisfied with this, he offers them his daughter's short and sweet counter-narrative: the red represents passion and the white virginity. They confront each other in a forest of phallic symbols.

Allow me to add my own Rauschenberg story, a tale that leads us back once again to Albers and Hofmann. Rauschenberg studied with Albers at Black Mountain College in 1948 and 1949. Years later, he recalled the difficult relationship with his mentor:

> I'm still learning what he taught me, because what he taught me had to do with the entire visual world. He didn't teach you how to "do art." The focus was always on your personal sense of looking. I consider Albers the most important teacher I've ever had, and I'm sure he considers me one of his poorest students.[23]

Rauschenberg may not have done the exercises properly, but he learned that any material could be used for art (Albers was very open-minded on this score) and that any exercise, however structured, had to be personal. Seen this way, *Archive*'s catholic inclusion of techniques and sources is pure Albers. And yet, despite Rauschenberg's insistence on Albers's influence, the formal and visual qualities of *Archive* have just as much to do with Hofmann—the broad palette (blue, yellow, red, green, white, brown); the push and pull of rectangles and color patches in shallow space; the combination of thick and flat areas, of geometry and gesture. The Meyerhoffs acquired *Archive* in 1963, the year it was painted. It was one of their first paintings by a young artist, a member of the post–Abstract Expressionist generation, and it held what would become the poles of their collection—abstraction and representation, geometry and gesture, exuberance and reticence—in remarkable balance (fig. 9).

Whereas Johns's *Perilous Night* jams competing, hermetic systems of notation and reference up against one another, Rauschenberg's *Archive* offers breathing space, possibilities of slippage, trains of association. The genius of *Archive* is that it stimulates different accounts of itself and allows them to coexist. The three stories that I have told about it are equally plausible, and equally fantastic. Rauschenberg's rectangles are not visually flattening (although they can be that) as much as hermeneutically leveling. They are democratic. Take your pick, or propose another story—the road is open.

[1] Jane Meyerhoff, "The Collector's Perspective," in *The Robert and Jane Meyerhoff Collection: 1958–1979*, ed. Nina C. Sundell (Baltimore: Baltimore Museum of Art, 1980), n.p.

[2] Hillel the Elder, *Babylonian Talmud*, tractate Shabbat 31a, cited in "Hillel the Elder," *Wikipedia*, accessed December 11, 2013, http://en.wikipedia.org/wiki/Hillel-The-Elder.

[3] Jane Meyerhoff, "Collector's Statement," in Mark Rosenthal, ed., *The Robert and Jane Meyerhoff Collection: 1945–1995*, exh. cat. (Washington, DC: National Gallery of Art, 1996), 11.

[4] Jackson Pollock, handwritten note, 1950, quoted in David Anfam, *Abstract Expressionism* (London: Thames & Hudson, 1990), 121; Pollock, interview with William Wright, 1951, quoted in Elizabeth Frank, *Jackson Pollock* (New York: Abbeville Press, 1983), 110.

[5] Clement Greenberg, "After Abstract Expressionism" (1962), in *The Collected Essays and Criticism*, vol. 4: *Modernism with a Vengeance, 1957–1969*, ed. John O'Brian (Chicago and London: University of Chicago Press, 1993), 131.

[6] Maurice Denis, "Definition of Neo-Traditionalism" (1890), in *Art in Theory, 1815–1900: An Anthology of Changing Ideas*, eds. Charles Harrison and Paul Wood (London: Blackwell, 1998), 863. Denis regarded Sérusier's *Talisman* (fig. 1) as the epitome of his formalist ideas.

[7] Hans Hofmann, "The Resurrection of the Plastic Arts" (1954), repr. in Sam Hunter, *Hans Hofmann* (New York: Harry N. Abrams, 1963), 44–45.

[8] Here Hofmann draws on the lesson of the Fauves, who had magnified Seurat's points into discrete strokes or patches of single colors while maintaining his interest in the juxtaposition of complements. For a classic example, see Henri Matisse's *Open Window, Collioure*, 1905 (National Gallery of Art, Washington).

[9] Jane Meyerhoff, in conversation with Robert Meyerhoff and Irving Blum, National Gallery of Art, Washington, East Building Auditorium, March 31, 1996.

[10] I use the word *concentric* somewhat loosely. The squares of the *Homages* (whether the three- or four-square format) do not share the same center; as the squares get smaller, the centers get lower, although they are all located on the vertical midline of the panel. I also use the word *nested* loosely: each *Homage* is composed of a single square surrounded by square frames, with no overlapping paint.

[11] Josef Albers, quoted in Katharine Kuh, *The Artist's Voice: Talks with Seventeen Artists* (New York: Da Capo Press, 1962), 11.

[12] The poem is reproduced in *Josef Albers*, exh. cat. (Raleigh: North Carolina Museum of Art, 1962), 11.

[13] Albers to Margit Rowell, 1971, in Rowell, "On Albers' Color," *Artforum* 10 (January 1972): 27.

[14] Ibid., 36.

[15] Clement Greenberg, *Hofmann* (Paris: G. Fall, 1961), 28–34; Michael Fried, "New York Letter: Hofmann" (1963), repr. in Fried, *Art and Objecthood: Essays and Reviews* (Chicago and London: University of Chicago Press, 1998), 295.

[16] Hans Hofmann, statement in the catalogue of a 1955 exhibition, Samuel M. Kootz Gallery, New York, repr. in Barbara Rose, *Readings in American Art, 1900–1975* (New York: Praeger, 1975), 117.

[17] Hofmann Lectures (winter 1938–1939), lecture IV, p. 6, typescript in Clement Greenberg Papers, Getty Research Institute, box 26, folder 10, cited in Michael Schreyach, "Re-Created Flatness: Hans Hofmann's Concept of the Picture Plane as a Medium of Expression," *Journal of Aesthetic Education*, 48, no. 3 (fall 2014).

[18] Early version cited in Judith Oster, *Toward Robert Frost: The Reader and the Poet* (Athens: University of Georgia Press, 1991), 226.

[19] Clement Greenberg, "Review of an Exhibition of Hans Hofmann," in *The Collected Essays and Criticism*, vol. 2: *Arrogant Purpose, 1945–1949*, ed. John O'Brian (Chicago and London: University of Chicago Press, 1986), 18.

[20] Cf. Clement Greenberg, "Collage" (1959), in *Art and Culture: Critical Essays* (Boston: Beacon Press, 1961), 71, where he describes the space of Analytic Cubist paintings as "sealed between two parallel flatnesses—the depicted Cubist flatness and the literal flatness of the paint surface."

[21] Additionally, they are one and the same boy, evidently the same left-handed model, who is posed differently in different suits. Likewise, the young girls at left and right are twins, if not identical. Pairing begins to seem to be the logic of the picture, a logic that is rudely ruptured by the amputee approaching us from the back of the scene, who lacks a complete pair of arms.

[22] Rosalind E. Krauss, "Grids" (1978), repr. in *The Originality of the Avant-Garde and Other Modernist Myths* (Cambridge, MA, and London: MIT Press, 1986), 9–22.

[23] Robert Rauschenberg, interview with John Stix, 1972, quoted in *Josef Albers: A Retrospective*, ed. Diane Waldman, exh. cat. (New York: Solomon R. Guggenheim Museum, 1988), 55.

PLATES

All works of art are from the National Gallery of Art, Washington, Collection of Robert and Jane Meyerhoff, unless otherwise noted.

BARNETT NEWMAN
AMERICAN, 1905–1970

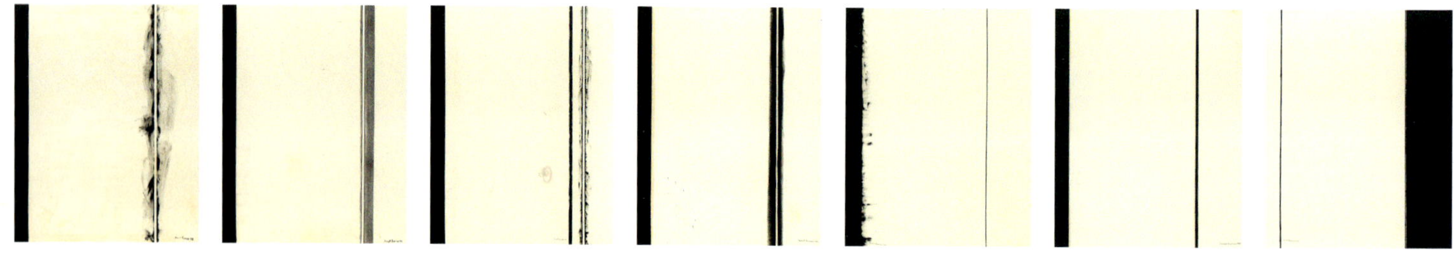

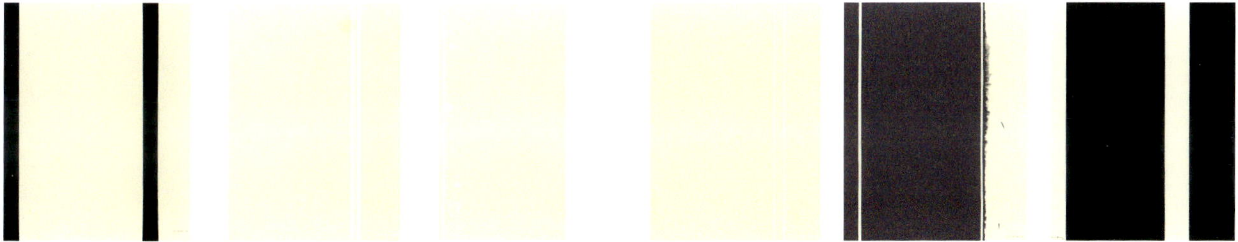

Barnett Newman, *The Stations of the Cross: Lema Sabachthani*, 1958–1966 (pls. 1–15)

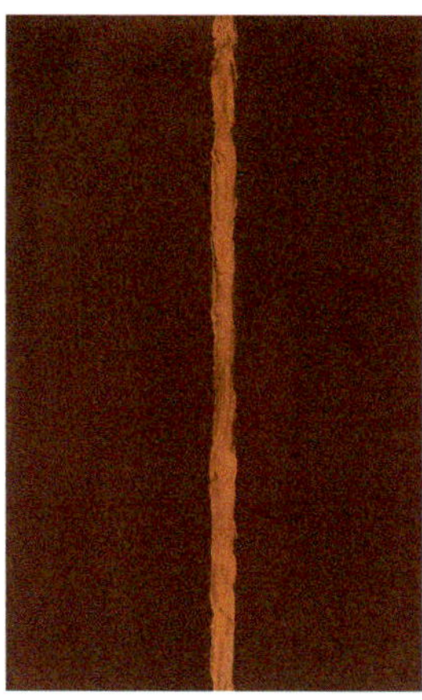

Fig. 10: Barnett Newman, *Onement I*, 1948. Oil on canvas and oil on masking tape on canvas, 27 1/4 x 16 1/8 in. (69.2 x 41.2 cm). The Museum of Modern Art, New York, Gift of Annalee Newman, 390.1992

Born in New York City, Barnett Newman took drawing classes during his senior year of high school at the Art Students League, where he became close friends with the painter Adolph Gottlieb, and then studied philosophy at City College. Working in his father's clothing business before and after the Crash of 1929, he turned increasingly to art as an aspiring teacher in the city's public schools (he failed the exam four times), a writer, a critic, and a practitioner. In the 1930s, he grew close to Milton Avery and Mark Rothko, although he later destroyed the Expressionist works he had made during this period. The first pieces that Newman judged worthy of preservation were his Surrealist-inspired works on paper and occasional paintings from the 1940s, displaying biomorphic forms (he was studying botany and ornithology) and the experimental and suggestive use of materials such as ink and crayon. The images in Newman's art became more abstract and minimal as his breakthrough approached.

In 1948, at the age of forty-three, Newman painted *Onement I* (fig. 10). The structure of the small work was simple: a smoothly brushed, allover field of Indian red; a piece of masking tape stretching from top to bottom of the canvas and dividing it equally; and a thick, uneven line of cadmium red light, applied with a palette knife over the tape. Newman had used tape before to help create edges and to mask areas temporarily, so, after testing out the cadmium color on top of it, he probably planned to remove the tape and paint the strip of canvas under it with that color—but he did not. Instead, he was stopped in his tracks by what he saw, and he studied it for months before starting anything else. A productive burst followed, with eighteen paintings completed in 1949, his most prolific year ever.

As its redundant title insists, *Onement I* was Newman's breakthrough, his self-declared origin point. He claimed that he had painted it on his forty-third birthday. His previous abstractions had been full of brushy atmosphere; *Onement I* was his first to risk a flat, unmodulated field of color. And, although he had been using stripes in his paintings and drawings for three years, it was the first to use the "zip," as he later called it, as a crucial element. (Perhaps thinking of zippers, Newman insisted that his zips did not divide but unified his works.)[1] For an artist who had explored Surrealism earlier in the decade but could not quite find himself, this simple painting answered the central question of what he called the "moral crisis" after World War II: "What are we going to paint?"[2]

Fast-forward ten years to 1958; Newman was despondent. The same decade that brought glory to his Abstract Expressionist colleagues, from Jackson Pollock to Mark Rothko to Willem de Kooning, was passing Newman by, leaving him virtually unnoticed. His last exhibition, at the Betty Parsons Gallery in 1951, had been a commercial failure, and he had withdrawn from the public eye. A slow and deliberate worker, he painted some major works in 1954 and 1955, but completed nothing in 1956 and 1957. Short of money, he frequented the racetrack and tried unsuccessfully to sue

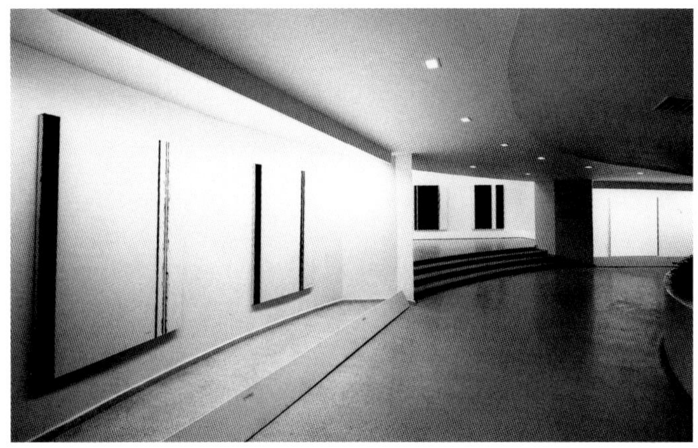

Fig. 11: Paul Katz, Barnett Newman's *The Stations of the Cross* at the Solomon R. Guggenheim Museum, New York, 1966. Paul Katz Archive, Department of Image Collections, National Gallery of Art Library, Washington

Ad Reinhardt for libel over critical comments he had made about Newman in *Art Journal*. In late 1957, he suffered a major heart attack.

It was in early 1958, while recovering from his heart attack, that Newman stretched the first two of what would become *The Stations of the Cross: Lema Sabachthani*, a series of consecutively numbered canvases, all nearly identical in size. In 1966, he recalled, "From the very beginning I felt that I would do a series." And it was while working on the fourth painting in 1960, he said, that he began to "think of them as the Stations of the Cross."[3] Their palette was limited to black, battleship gray (in the *Twelfth Station*), white, and the color of the raw canvas. After eight years of intermittent but intense work, including a burst of five paintings in 1965–1966, he showed the fourteen paintings, along with a kind of coda titled *Be II*, by themselves at the Solomon R. Guggenheim Museum, New York, in 1966—Newman's first solo show in a museum (fig. 11). He planned the installation and chose the title, *The Stations of the Cross: Lema Sabachthani*, the Aramaic words of Jesus's cry from the cross, "Why have you forsaken me?"

Perhaps it was a sense of mortality following his heart attack, as well as some personal identification with the sufferings of Christ, that stimulated Newman to embark on such a project. No doubt Rothko's work on an ensemble of dark paintings for the Four Seasons Restaurant in the Seagram Building, which began in 1957, was also on Newman's competitive mind. But the immediate source for the theme of the *Stations* seems to have been his friend Tony Smith, the architect and painter, who had written to Newman from Germany (where Smith had moved in 1953) about a "church idea" in which "paintings would play an integral part." In particular, as Smith wrote in a formal proposal that he circulated to artists and architects, he envisioned the art as a set of fourteen abstract paintings symbolic in number and position of the Stations of the Cross. The church project never attracted a patron, but in a sense Newman began to make the art for it five years later.[4] Indeed, there is evidence that the theme of the *Stations* had occurred to Newman from the very start of the series rather than in 1960 as he claimed: his first painting following the heart attack, a narrow vertical work with a wide, expressively brushed zip, was titled *Outcry* (1958), evoking the cry that Newman regarded as central to the content of the *Stations*.[5]

Comparing the *Stations* with the earlier *Onement I* shows just how far Newman had traveled from his breakthrough to the most ambitious work of his maturity: from singularity to multiplicity; from small to large scale; from a fairly simple, instrumental use of masking tape to subtle effects of bleeding-under and brushing-over; and from a transfixing central symmetry to an ever-shifting laterality.

It is this last development that art historian Yve-Alain Bois identifies as the crucial one of Newman's career. The eureka of *Onement I*, argues Bois, was the artist's realization that bilateral symmetry in painting, with its similarity to the body of the viewer, achieved a direct,

Fig. 12: Barnett Newman, *Yellow Painting*, 1949. Oil on canvas, 67 1/2 x 52 3/8 in. (171.4 x 133.1 cm). National Gallery of Art, Washington, Gift of Annalee Newman, in Honor of the 50th Anniversary of the National Gallery of Art

present-tense mode of address that at once unified the canvas and gave the beholder a fixed place in front of it. In other words—very different words—*Onement I* embodied the "Here I am" with which biblical figures from Abraham to Isaiah declared their presence to God, often at moments of tension or tragedy.[6] The work established, at however small a scale, what Newman called *makom* (Hebrew for "place," with strong overtones of the sacred), thus furthering the ambition that the artist shared with his Abstract Expressionist colleagues: to make paintings that carried profound meanings, not via narrative or depiction, but somehow through form and color themselves, in their relationship to the viewer.

• • •

In the works that immediately followed *Onement I*, Newman had explored the impact of bilateral symmetry at a larger scale, in different colors, with different numbers and widths of zip. *Yellow Painting*, of 1949 (fig. 12), includes two white zips near the edges of a yellow field and a central zip of subtly different yellow at center. But the symmetrical formula had its limits. Never one to repeat himself too closely, Newman "began to realize that what was essential for him in bilateral symmetry was less the central axis and the self-duplication—the 'bi'—than the *laterality*, the lateral extension."[7] And so the revelation of *Onement I* soon opened into widely spreading horizontal canvases with irregularly placed zips, such as *Vir Heroicus Sublimis* (1950–1951), and ultimately into the *Stations*, which can be regarded as Newman's largest single work.

If works like *Onement I* trigger the ringing statement "Here I am," then the *Stations* might seem to raise the question "Where am I?" Is my proper place in front of each of the paintings, one by one, or walking by them, or turning around in the middle of the room to try to take in the series as a whole? For that matter, am I in an art gallery at all, or, as the title suggests, am I passing by the Stations on the road to Calvary?

It is not clear when Newman decided on the series' title, but when he revealed it to Lawrence Alloway, the curator of the Guggenheim exhibition, just a few months before the opening, it came as a shock.[8] One can imagine several reasons for this. First, Newman was not a believing Christian but a secular Jew; when choosing biblical titles for previous paintings, he had favored the Old Testament. Second, the Stations of the Cross is not a major theme in the history of painting, even representational painting: most often it is represented by relief sculptures or paintings placed low around the nave of a church for worshippers to walk by, emulating pilgrims on the actual Via Dolorosa in Jerusalem. Few of these are considered masterpieces. But, above all, the title seems to be at odds with Newman's fundamental belief in the power of abstract art to carry meaning on its own, for it immediately suggests an analogy between the fourteen paintings and the fourteen locations where, in Roman Catholic liturgy, Jesus stopped on his journey from receiving his death sentence to being laid in his tomb. Even Henri Matisse's *Stations of the Cross* (1948–1951), on the back wall of his chapel at Vence (fig. 13), the major

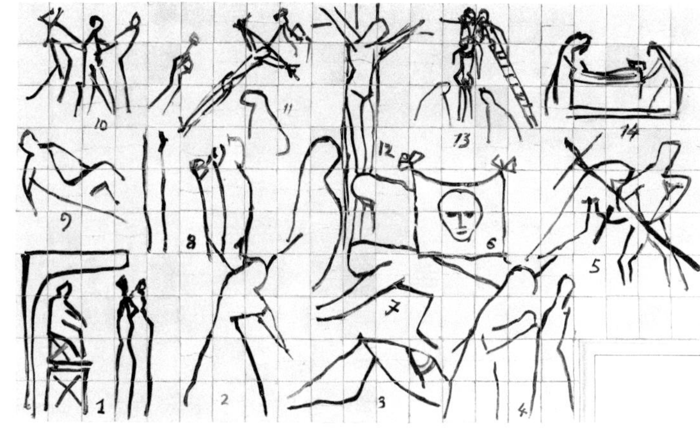

Fig. 13: Henri Matisse, *Stations of the Cross*, 1948–1951. Ceramic tile in the nave of the Chapel of the Rosary, Vence, France

modern precedent for Newman's subject, told a clear story in its numbered scenes, despite its simple and abstracted monochromatic drawing.

Newman was crucified in the press for what was seen as the absurdity and pretension of the implied analogy between the actual Stations and his paintings. Anticipating just such a response, he had prepared a statement that was published in *ARTnews* during the exhibition: "Just as the Passion is not a series of anecdotes but embodies a single event, so these fourteen paintings, even though each one is whole and separate in its immediacy, all together form a complete statement of a single subject."[9] And that single subject was the cry signaled in Newman's subtitle, as he explained in the small catalogue for the exhibition: "*Lema Sabachthani*—why? Why did you forsake me? . . . This is the Passion. This outcry of Jesus. Not the terrible walk up the Via Dolorosa, but the question that has no answer."[10] In other words, Newman suggested, there was no one-to-one correspondence between the paintings and the Stations, because the Stations were essentially one thing, just as his series was one thing—and that one thing was "the story of each man's agony," an "unanswerable cry" that had as much to do with Job, with everyman, as with Jesus.[11] Thus Newman attempted (without much success) to forestall both the generally narrative as well as the specifically Christian reading of the work suggested by its title.

Where does that leave us? Newman's words hint that the meaning of the work has more to do with existential tragedy than with any one particular story, and that our viewing, while respecting the integrity of each of the paintings, should attempt to synthesize them into a whole. But such a viewing is easier said than done. One commentator has suggested that Newman's discontinuous installation of the *Stations* at the Guggenheim (the first four paintings were displayed along the spiral ramp and the next ten in a more conventional gallery off the ramp) was meant to emphasize the successiveness of the experience, and to require an act of memory in order to synthesize it.[12] But the architecture of Frank Lloyd Wright's museum presented a unique challenge, and we do not know Newman's feelings about this (although he was delighted with the exhibition as a whole). Another commentator has remarked that the apparently unintentional drips and splashes that Newman surprisingly left visible on the edges of the paintings—a feature that cannot be seen from the front, only obliquely—may be a device to keep the gaze, and the feet, moving, especially given that most of the marks are on the left and so lead the viewer through a standard left-to-right installation.[13] Such readings take Newman's memorable "I was a pilgrim as I painted" literally, and conclude that the viewer, too, should approach the paintings as a pilgrim, moving past them in order.[14]

It is equally important, of course, to spend time with each work, ignoring the pull of the series. The fact that the compositions of the paintings are so similar—each one except for the fourteenth is built around two vertical divisions, one about five inches from the left edge, the other about fifteen inches from the right—creates continuity through the series, as if performing an act of memory for us. That continuity makes it possible for us to appreciate all the changes that Newman rings on the theme—all the variations of technique and material, all the different treatments of edge and surface. Newman's unusually prominent (for him) signature on each work provides further continuity, while the changing date announces that the series was done over time, as our viewing must be. Despite all the continuity, the paintings, Newman insisted, are each "whole and separate."[15]

Clearly, this wholeness is nothing like that of *Yellow Painting* or any of the rivetingly symmetrical compositions that followed in the wake of *Onement I*. Instead of a central zip, we are given bands of varying widths. These are always peripheral (especially so in the "coda" painting, *Be II*), suggesting that Newman was after a splitting of vision—not just in the challenge posed by the multi-part nature of the series as a whole, but in each of its members. It is this very emphasis on peripheral rather than focal vision, obliquity rather than frontality, that the mature Newman embraced as a more profound way to achieve the "Here I am" than he had won, perhaps too easily, with *Onement I*. What Bois writes of another work by Newman applies as well to each of the *Stations* and to the whole cycle: "We never manage to take in everything simultaneously, and the only things we are able to grasp with certitude in front of such a vacillating image are, when we step back, the lateral expanse of the whole canvas and its more-than-human height."[16] If this throws us back on our perceiving body, making us self-aware in front of the work (*here*), it also makes us perceive each painting in the undivided fullness that Newman craved. These two things are directly connected: it is only by abandoning the hope of visual mastery, by letting ourselves just *be* in front of the painting, that we come to realize a fundamental axiom of modernism: "Everything in the painting counts."[17] And with the *Stations*, one might add, every painting counts.

The word "station" comes from the Latin *stare*, meaning "to stand." Perhaps this, at least in part, is the message of Newman's title: if we just take our place in front of the work, painting by painting, we will learn where we stand in relation to the whole.

HC

---

1 Barnett Newman, "Interview with Emile de Antonio" (1970), in John P. O'Neill, *Barnett Newman: Selected Writings and Interviews* (New York: Alfred A. Knopf, 1990), 302.

2 Ibid., 303.

3 Barnett Newman, "The Fourteen Stations of the Cross, 1958–1966," *ARTnews* 65, no. 3 (May 1966): 26–28, 57, repr. in O'Neill, *Barnett Newman*, 189.

4 Eileen Elizabeth Costello, "Beyond the Easel: The Dissolution of Abstract Expressionist Painting into the Realm of Architecture" (PhD diss., University of Texas at Austin, 2010), 135–137. Costello draws on letters and documents preserved in the Tony Smith Estate Archive.

5 However, the first recorded instance of the use of this title is in a letter, dated March 17, 1965, Newman wrote to curator Maurice Tuchman about an exhibition of New York School paintings at the Los Angeles County Museum, so it is possible that Newman did not come up with the title until then. My thanks to Heidi Colsman-Freyberger of the Barnett Newman Foundation for this information.

[6] Yve-Alain Bois, "Newman's Laterality," in *Reconsidering Barnett Newman*, ed. Melissa Ho (Philadelphia: Philadelphia Museum of Art, 2005), 41–42.

[7] Ibid., 34.

[8] Kathryn Tuma, "Reading Between the Lines: The Early History of Barnett Newman's *The Stations of the Cross*" (unpublished paper, 2005), 17.

[9] Newman, "The Fourteen Stations of the Cross," 190.

[10] Barnett Newman, "Statement," in *Barnett Newman: The Stations of the Cross, Lema Sabachthani*, exh. cat. (New York: Solomon R. Guggenheim Museum, 1966), repr. in O'Neill, *Barnett Newman*, 187–188. The fact that Newman here translates the cry with "did you forsake" rather than the traditional "have you forsaken" gives the question a tragic finality that may reflect his sense of the modern human predicament.

[11] Ibid., 188.

[12] Mark Godfrey, "Barnett Newman's 'Stations of the Cross' and the Memory of the Holocaust," in *Reconsidering Barnett Newman*, ed. Melissa Ho, 554–556.

[13] Sarah K. Rich, in conversation with the author. See her book *Past Flat: Other Sides to American Abstract Painting in the Cold War Era* (Berkeley and Los Angeles: University of California Press, 2014). Another explanation for the predominance of left-edge versus right-edge drippings is that most of the works have painted elements at the left edge but raw canvas at the right.

[14] Barnett Newman, interview in *Newsweek*, May 9, 1966, 100.

[15] Newman, "The Fourteen Stations of the Cross," 190.

[16] Bois, "Newman's Laterality," 36. Bois was discussing *Abraham* (1949).

[17] Ibid., 44.

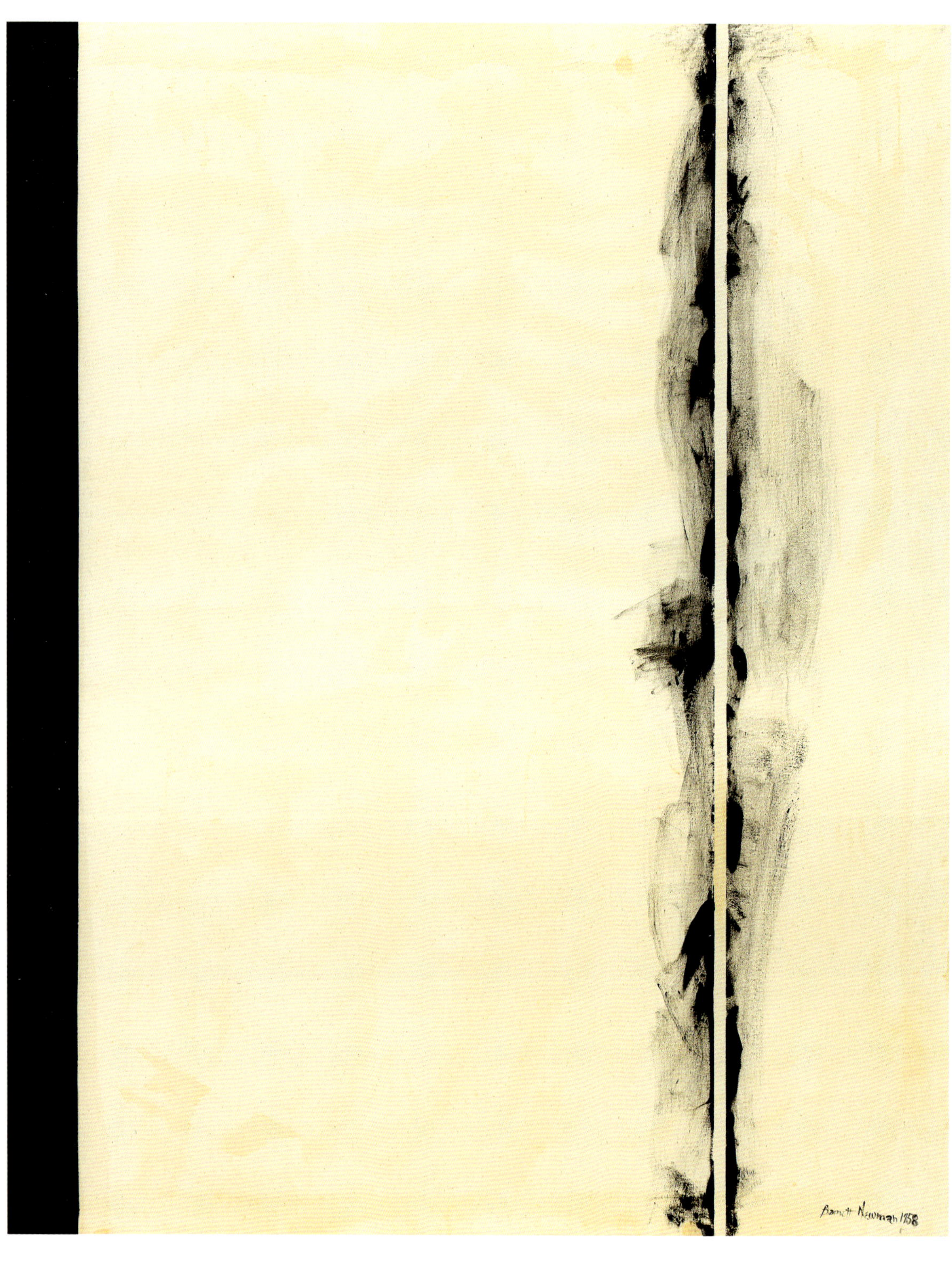

1. Barnett Newman, *First Station*, 1958. Magna on canvas, 77 7/8 x 60 1/2 in. (197.8 x 153.7 cm). 1986.65.1

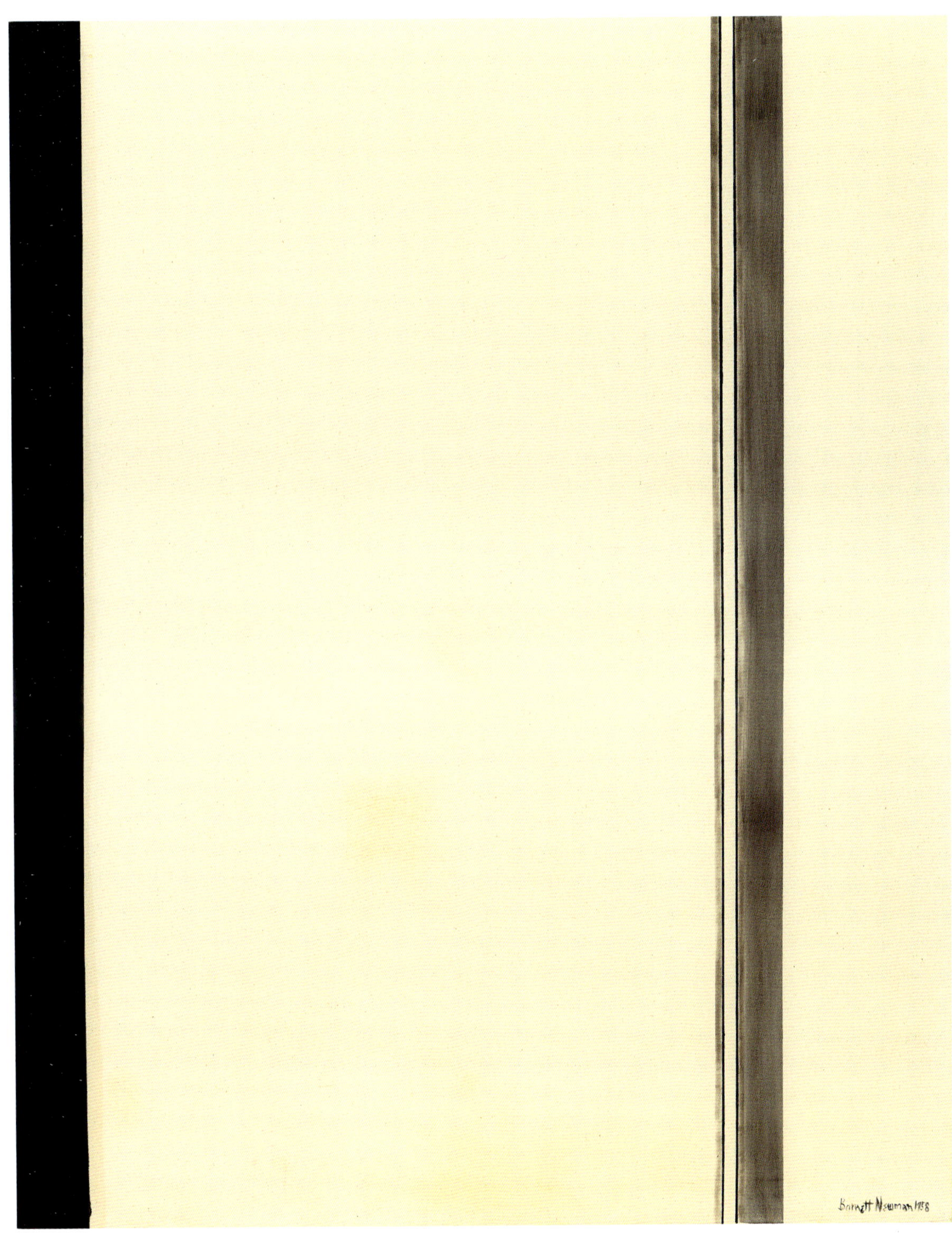

2. Barnett Newman, *Second Station*, 1958. Magna on canvas, 78 1/8 x 60 3/8 in. (198.4 x 153.2 cm). 1986.65.2

3. Barnett Newman, *Third Station*, 1960. Oil on canvas, 78 1/8 x 59 7/8 in. (198.4 x 152.1 cm). 1986.65.3

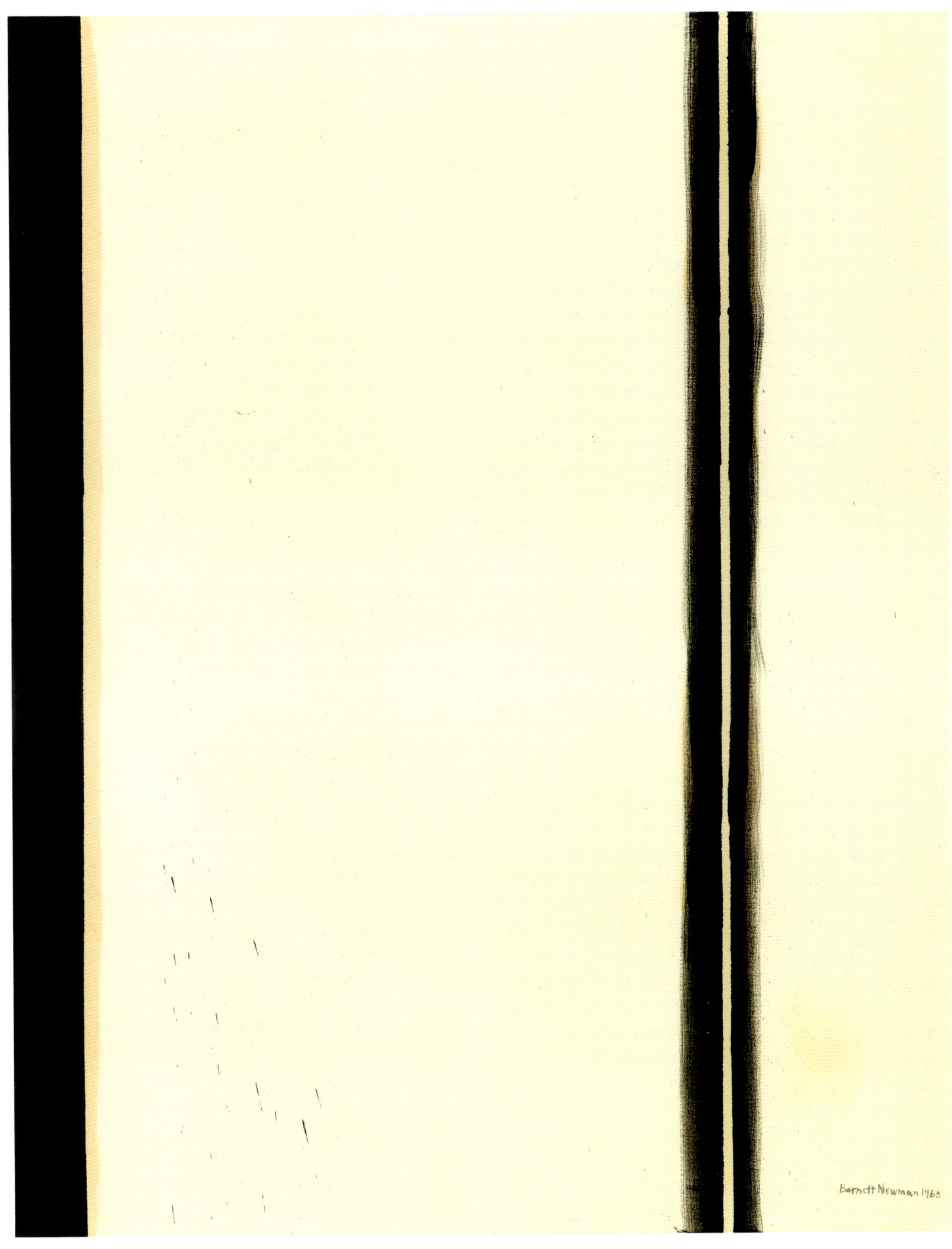

4. Barnett Newman, *Fourth Station*, 1960. Oil on canvas, 78 x 60 1/4 in. (198.1 x 153 cm). 1986.65.4

5. Barnett Newman, *Fifth Station*, 1962. Oil on canvas, 78 1/4 x 60 1/4 in. (198.7 x 153 cm). 1986.65.5

6. Barnett Newman, *Sixth Station,* 1962. Oil on canvas, 78 1/8 x 59 7/8 in. (198.4 x 152.1 cm). 1986.65.6

7. Barnett Newman, *Seventh Station*, 1964. Oil on canvas, 78 x 60 in. (198.1 x 152.4 cm). 1986.65.7

8. Barnett Newman, *Eighth Station*, 1964. Oil on canvas, 78 1/8 x 60 in. (198.4 x 152.4 cm). 1986.65.8

9. Barnett Newman, *Ninth Station*, 1964. Acrylic on canvas, 78 x 60 1/8 in. (198.1 x 152.7 cm). 1986.65.9

10. Barnett Newman, *Tenth Station*, 1965. Magna on canvas, 78 x 60 1/8 in. (198.1 x 152.5 cm). 1986.65.10

11. Barnett Newman, *Eleventh Station*, 1965. Acrylic on canvas, 78 x 60 in. (198.1 x 152.4 cm). 1986.65.11

12. Barnett Newman, *Twelfth Station*, 1965. Acrylic on canvas, 78 x 60 in. (198.1 x 152.4 cm). 1986.65.12

13. Barnett Newman, *Thirteenth Station*, 1965/1966. Acrylic on canvas, 78 1/8 x 60 1/8 in. (198.2 x 152.5 cm). 1986.65.13

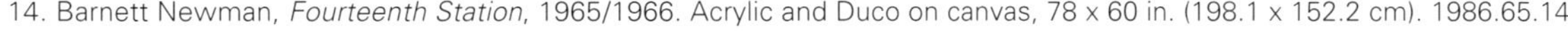

14. Barnett Newman, *Fourteenth Station*, 1965/1966. Acrylic and Duco on canvas, 78 x 60 in. (198.1 x 152.2 cm). 1986.65.14

15. Barnett Newman, *Be II*, 1961/1964. Acrylic and oil on canvas, 80 ½ x 72 ¼ in. (204.5 x 183.5 cm). 1986.65.15

JOSEF ALBERS

AMERICAN, b. GERMANY, 1888–1976

Study for Homage to the Square: Light Rising is a very early example of Josef Albers's best-known work, the *Homage to the Square* series, which he began in 1950 and continued developing with many variations until his death in 1976. The *Homages* would eventually comprise more than one thousand works, including drawings, paintings, prints, and textiles. Before arriving at this groundbreaking series, Albers had spent time at the Bauhaus, Black Mountain College, and Yale University School of Art, where he honed his skills as both a teacher and a writer while continuing to develop as a visual artist.

The *Homages* are defined by a basic format of three or four squares nested within each other, creating bands of juxtaposed color in varying sizes. The squares act as a neutral form, allowing color relationships to take center stage, yet the arrangements hum with subtle energy. The squares of color advance outward but at the same time recede inward; either reading is possible. The implied diagonals within each block add to the energy and sharpen the corners. No outlines define the planes of color, which allows them to interact freely and directly with each other.

Albers first primed his panels with white to give luminosity to the whole. He generally worked with oil paints straight from the tube, leached of some of their oil and laid down with flicks of the palette knife rather than a brush. In this work, the inner square is pale barium yellow. Next comes the largest area of color, a warm gray, which is enveloped, in turn, by a shade of whitened blue. The gray was applied with sharper strokes of the knife, allowing the white priming layer to shine through. Despite its title, the painting is a finished, autonomous work, not a study for something else: Albers often qualified his titles with the word *study* to underscore his commitment to investigation and research.

Albers was largely concerned with light as a property of color. In his renowned teaching text, *Interaction of Color* (1963), he describes how distinctions dissolve when colors of equal value are juxtaposed. "Thus, the boundaries between grey and blue vanish, and we do not see where clouds end and where sky begins. With such clouds, this is best observed with the sun at our backs."[1] Here, the interaction of yellow, gray, and blue and the orientation of the squares create a similar effect, radiating and glowing, except that the yellow sun is not at our backs but in our eyes.

PR

[1] Josef Albers, *Interaction of Color* (New Haven: Yale University Press, 1971 [1963]), 64.

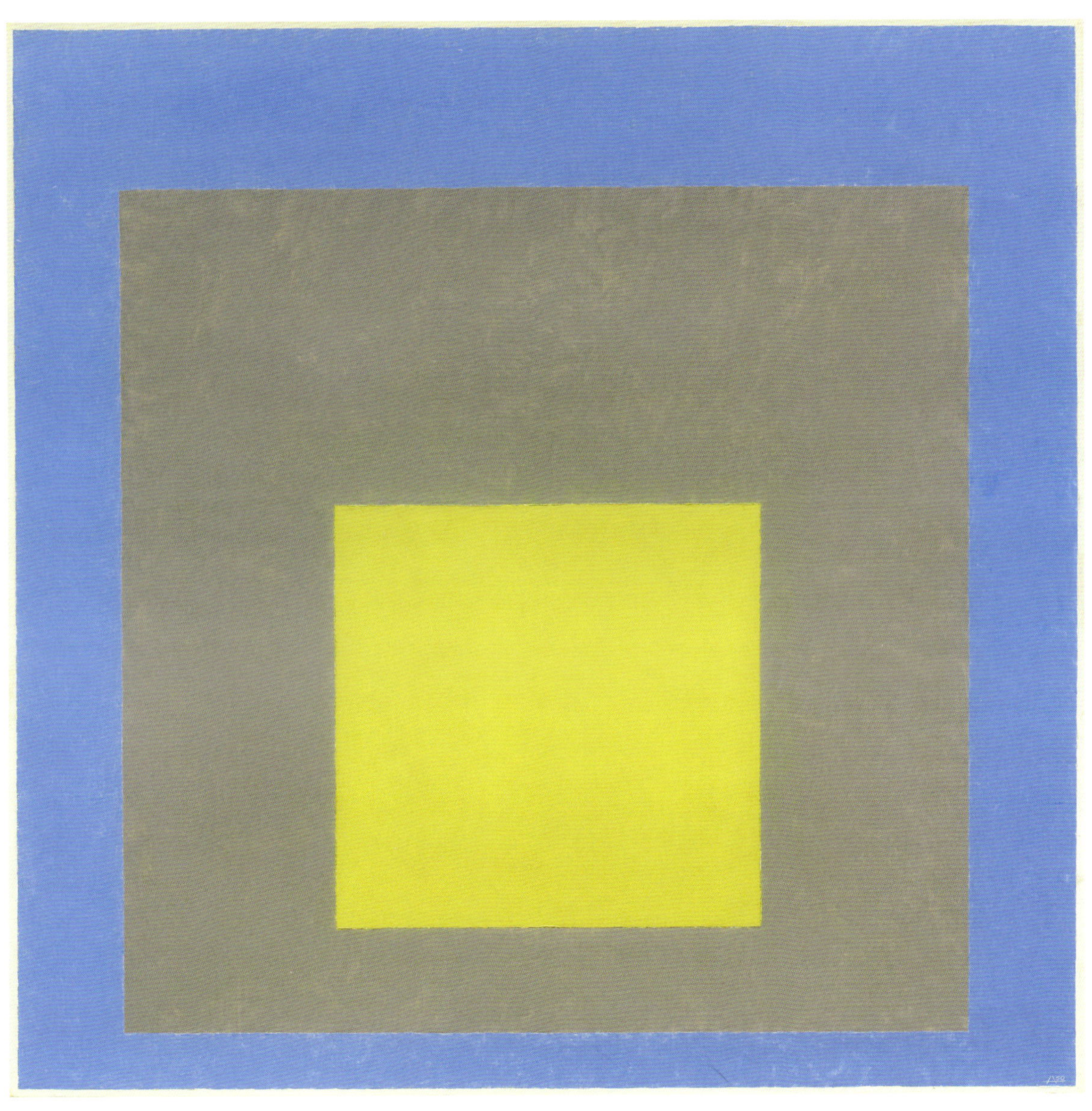

16. Josef Albers, *Study for Homage to the Square: Light Rising*, 1950, altered 1959. Oil on wood fiberboard, 32 x 32 in. (81.3 x 81.3 cm). 1992.28.1

WILLIAM BAZIOTES

AMERICAN, 1912–1963

While living in New York City in the early 1940s, William Baziotes frequented the Museum of Natural History, with its myriad displays of fossils and specimens. He also met many major figures of the Surrealist movement who had fled Europe for New York before and during World War II. Their example prompted him to use biomorphic forms that looked as if they had stepped out of a dream. These figures are crude and delicate at once, inspired by both observation and unconscious thoughts. Baziotes was also stimulated by Surrealist experiments with automatism and improvisation: he rarely composed a work in advance, instead letting his hands and the materials take over. The painting evolved freely and naturally until the subject was at last revealed. In this Baziotes had much in common with his bold Abstract Expressionist colleagues, yet, like Bradley Walker Tomlin, he retained a delicacy and lyricism that distinguished him within the group.

By the 1950s, Baziotes's work had become less abstract. *Desert Landscape* consists of three biomorphic shapes floating in a pale ocher background alive with underlying tints. This tan space suggests an ancient wilderness, be it a scene of origins or an ancestral burial ground. The brown and yellow forms are enigmatic: they evoke fossils, mythological phantoms, or even extraterrestrial creatures. The jagged tail and triangular scales of the yellow figure recall a dinosaur.

Baziotes mixed painting and drawing techniques within this work. The forms are outlined with charcoal and filled with paint, creating flat shapes—but not everything is as simple as it appears. In the ovoid at left, a thin charcoal line establishes the form while blotches of pink and lavender paint glow beyond its edge, illuminating the landscape like a soft beacon. Thinly applied layers of oil paint spread a glimmering phosphoric atmosphere throughout, with iridescent pinks and purples enshrouding the forms like a fog. Revealing his Surrealist side, Baziotes exclaimed, "It is the mysterious that I love in painting. It is the stillness and the silence. I want my pictures to take effect very slowly, to obsess and to haunt."[1]

PR

---

[1] William Baziotes, "Notes on Painting," *It Is.*, no. 4 (Autumn 1959): 11.

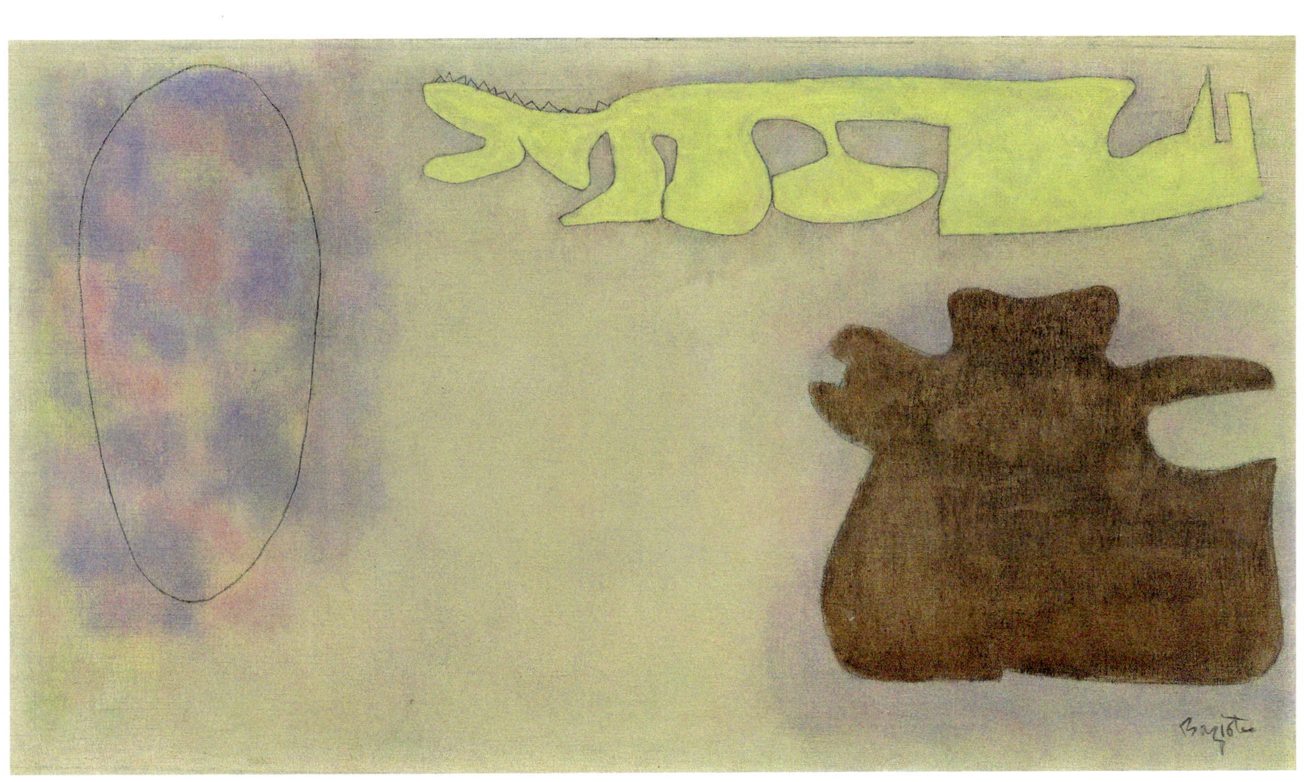

17. William Baziotes, *Desert Landscape*, 1951. Oil and charcoal on canvas, 24 1/8 x 42 in. (61.3 x 106.7 cm). 1996.81.1

ANTHONY CARO

BRITISH, 1924–2013

Anthony Caro was born in Surrey, near London, and studied engineering at Christ's College, Cambridge, before he was conscripted into the British Navy. After studying sculpture at Regent Street Polytechnic and the Royal Academy schools in London, he worked as a part-time assistant to British sculptor Henry Moore from 1951 to 1953.

Caro began his professional career as a sculptor by modeling clay. He was still working in a figurative mode in 1959 when he received a Ford Foundation grant to visit the United States. Before leaving, he met the visiting American critic Clement Greenberg, whose comments on his work, he would recall, "shook me to my roots."[1] In the United States, Caro met the sculptor David Smith and saw an exhibition of Kenneth Noland's early Target paintings at French & Company in New York. Upon his return to England, Caro began to make abstract, planar, brightly painted metal constructions in his garage. This new body of work was featured in his first solo exhibition, at the Whitechapel Gallery in London in 1963. These sculptures challenged Moore's organic abstraction, while also presenting an alternative to the simple, unitary compositions of the burgeoning Minimalist movement. The positive reaction of American critics, particularly Greenberg and Michael Fried, brought the work great attention and secured its influence on younger artists.

These sculptures of the early 1960s were relatively large and sat directly upon the ground. In 1966, however, Caro became engaged by the problem of making small-scale sculptures that would sit upon bases or pedestals. He began to assemble disparate fragments scavenged from the scrapyard or left over from larger works. That was when, Caro recalled, he "came to realize [in conversation with Fried] that there was something special about the table, that is the table's edge."[2] To prevent these small pieces from looking like maquettes of his larger work, Caro made them table-specific: their overhanging elements (a universal feature of the group) defy the floor, which precludes the sculptures' "transportation, in fact or in imagination, to the ground."[3] William Rubin argues that the suggestion of handles in many of the works fixes their small scale in inherent relation to the body.[4]

Table Piece LXX is composed of five steel elements, each welded to another at a single point so that the sculpture extends laterally. At one end, a curved metal bar hangs below the edge of the base, providing either a sharp terminus or a starting point for the sculpture. Caro balances this downward thrust with an upward-curving C shape at right. Between these bookends, a lively rhythm of opposition and accord unfolds.
KR

---

1 Anthony Caro, interviewed by Noel Chanan, September 1974, repr. in Ian Barker, *Anthony Caro: Quest for the New Sculpture* (London: Lund Humphries, 2004), 84. For Clement Greenberg on Caro, see Clement Greenberg, "Contemporary Sculpture: Anthony Caro," *Arts Yearbook* 8 (1965): 106–109.

2 Caro, quoted in Diane Waldman, *Anthony Caro* (New York: Abbeville Press, 1982), 66.

3 Michael Fried, "Caro's Abstractness," *Artforum* 9, no. 1 (September 1970): 32.

4 William Rubin, *Anthony Caro*, exh. cat. (New York: The Museum of Modern Art, 1975), 139.

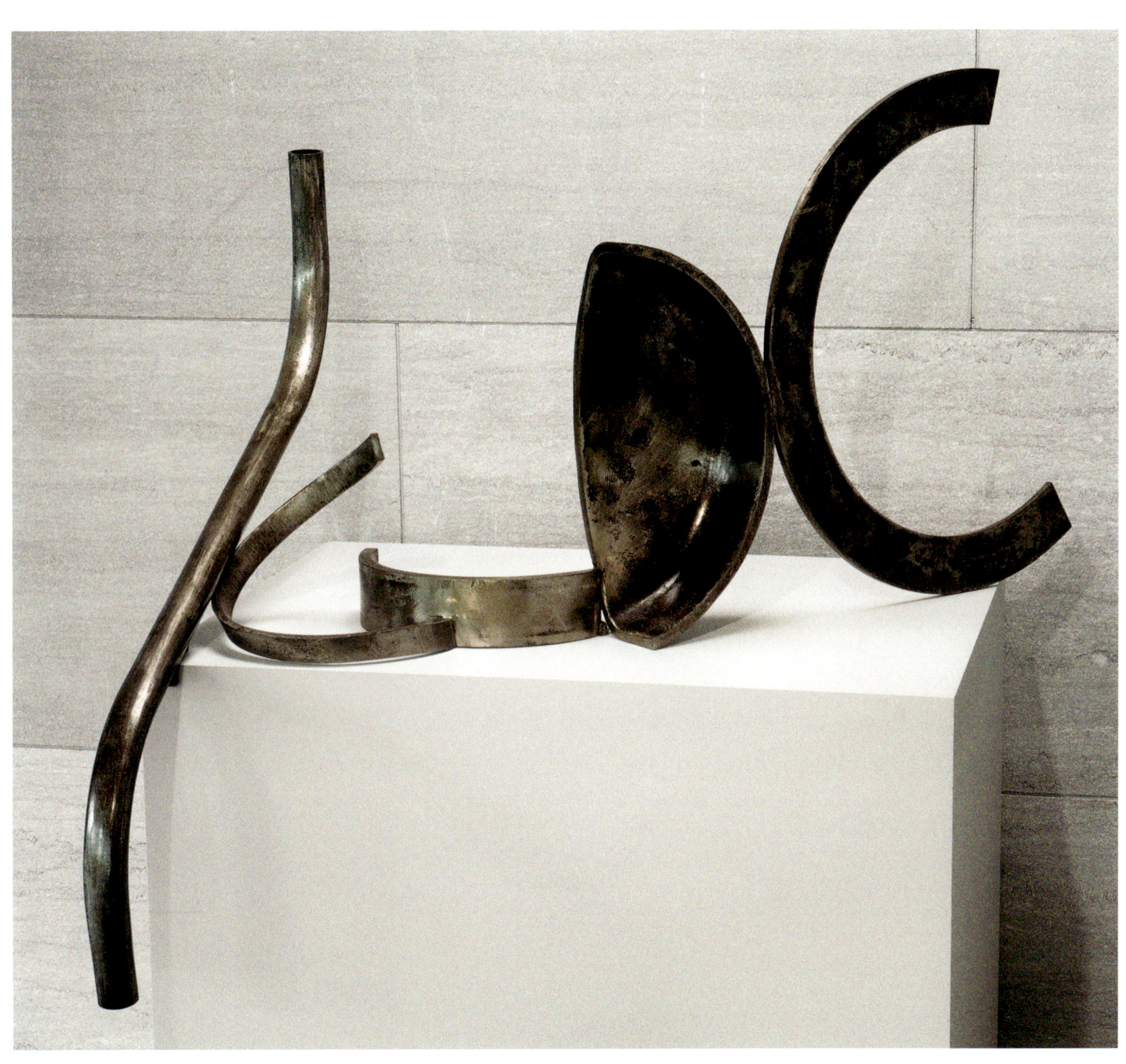

18. Anthony Caro, *Table Piece LXX*, 1968. Varnished steel, 33 1/2 x 51 x 25 in. (85.1 x 129.5 x 63.5 cm). 1992.28.9

JOSEPH CORNELL

AMERICAN, 1903–1972

Joseph Cornell transformed everyday materials into assemblages housed in glass-fronted boxes that showcase his unique vision of the world. A self-taught artist, he found inspiration in the sights and sounds around him—the movies, penny arcades, ballets, operas, and vaudeville shows he attended, as well as the skyscrapers, window displays, and street scenes he encountered while strolling in New York. In the 1920s, he began to frequent secondhand bookstores and antique shops in Lower Manhattan, collecting photographs, records, sheet music, trinkets, and baubles. This paraphernalia found its way into his early collages and film-related projects, and provided the substance for the boxes he began to make in 1932. Cornell also frequented the Julien Levy Gallery, where he discovered the Dada and Surrealist use of found objects, and where he would show his own works beginning in 1934. In 1936, Cornell constructed his first classic boxes, filling them with small objects to create a landscape of images and symbols.[1]

These boxes would occupy Cornell until his death in 1972. Their themes include the world of beauty (ballet, opera, Hollywood, works of art, jewels), doomed love, nature, time, astronomy, and the infinite. He often worked in series: aviaries, observatories, night skies/constellations, sand fountains, palaces, and dovecotes. The supplies at the artist's disposal included pipes, feathers, books, postage stamps, sand, maps, small bottles, corks, and marbles. Filled with mementos, sacred objects, and talismans, the boxes evoke Victorian parlors, reliquaries, and *Wunderkammern* (cabinets of curiosities in Renaissance Europe). They also stimulate a childish sense of wonder, owing both to their small size and the frequent inclusion of movable parts, which invite the viewer's involvement. An encounter with one of these objects is like a window onto a stage illuminated by remembrance, spreading nostalgia via Cornell's distinctive selection of materials.

Sand Fountain is an early work in a series employing sand that extended into the 1960s. The exterior of the box has a skin of faded pages from science and history books in Spanish, German, and French. An amber lacquer is used as a glaze, yellowing the material to feign aging. The inner sides of the box are lined with pieces of antique astronomical maps. Inside sits a broken cordial glass, half buried in yellow sand, whose shape recalls an hourglass. Above this glass is a white structure that resembles the keystone of an arch; in the middle of it is a dark circular aperture that contains minute specks of bright sand, like stars in the sky. When the box is inverted, the sand collects inside this structure; once the box is righted, the sand pours into the broken glass below, which begins to overflow. (The photograph reproduced here shows the box in action.) Runaway sand sprays out and builds up along the cracks and walls of the box. Once the sand stops, stillness takes over, suggesting time frozen. The fact that glass and sand have a shared chemistry magnifies the cosmic associations of the work.[2]

Les Constellations Voisines du Pôle is an example of Cornell's observatory boxes. A map of the stars is affixed to the back panel. Cornell sometimes used original prints of engraved maps and other times made Photostat copies that allowed him to use the same material in multiple works. In fact, *Les Constellations* and *Sand Fountain* incorporate some of the same images.[3] However, the diagrams in *Les Constellations* are larger, demonstrating how Cornell often played with the scale of his Photostats.

Les Constellations is more complex than it might first seem. It includes two parallel metal rods that run horizontally across the plane of the box. Atop these balances a painted white ball. One small brass ring hangs from the inner rod while two rings of equal size and a larger ring hang from the outer rod. Two small yellow cork balls roll on the floor, while seven white-painted nails stand guard in the lower right corner. Taken together, these elements imply both planetary motion and arcade games, both the cosmos and a microcosm.

PR

---

1 Lynda Roscoe Hartigan, *Joseph Cornell: Navigating the Imagination*, exh. cat. (Salem, MA: Peabody Essex Museum, 2007), 58–60.

2 Alexandra Cortesi, "Joseph Cornell," *Artforum* 4, no. 8 (April 1966): 29.

3 Nina C. Sundell, ed., *The Robert and Jane Meyerhoff Collection: 1958–1979* (Baltimore: Baltimore Museum of Art, 1980), 11.

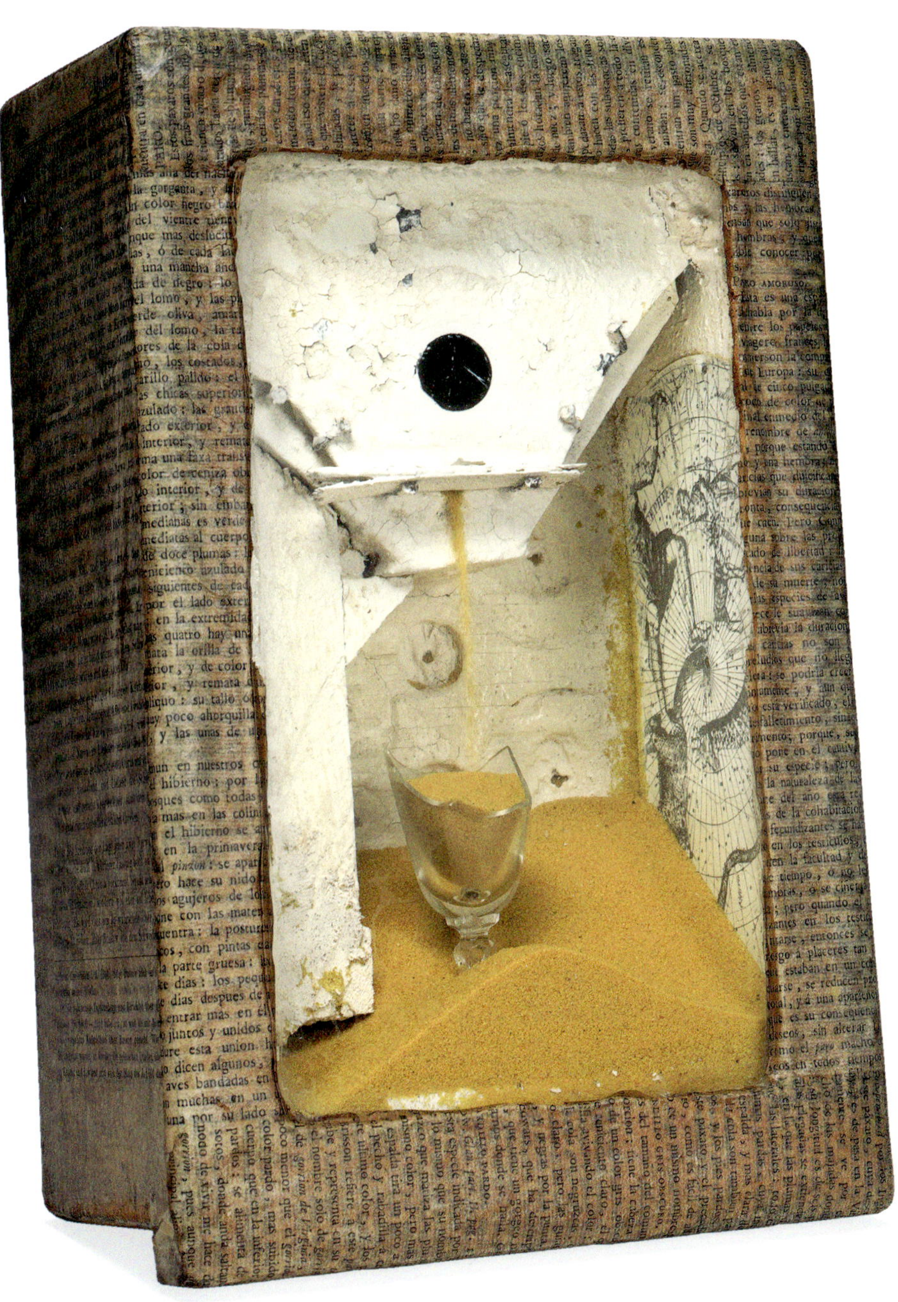

19. Joseph Cornell, *Sand Fountain*, 1948. Mixed-media construction, 11 x 7 x 4 in. (27.9 x 17.8 x 10.2 cm). 1991.218.1

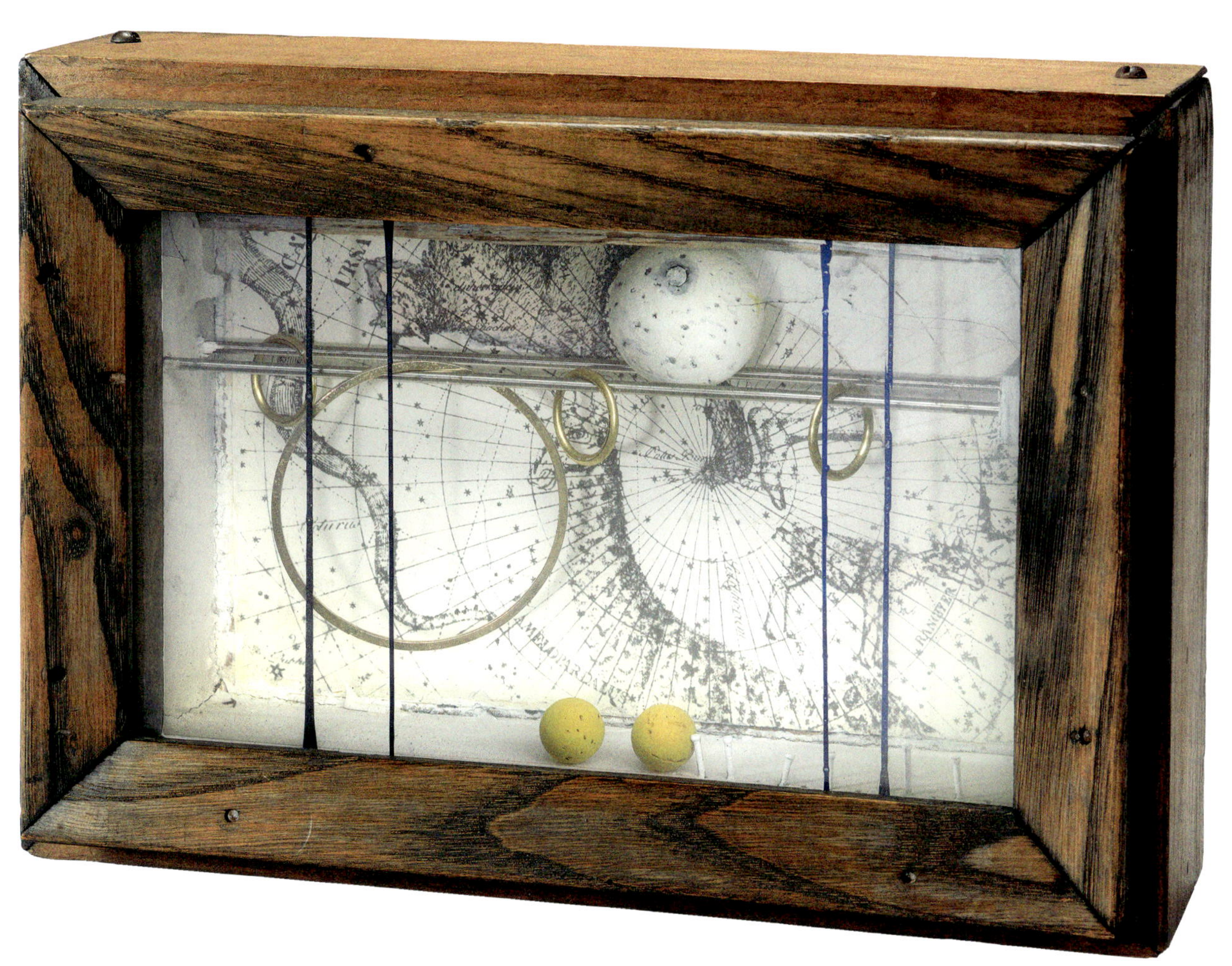

20. Joseph Cornell, *Les Constellations Voisines du Pôle*, 1961. Mixed-media construction, 8 x 11 x 2 in. (20.3 x 27.9 x 5.1 cm). 1991.218.2

BURGOYNE DILLER

AMERICAN, 1906–1965

Burgoyne Diller was one of the first American artists to adopt the abstract geometric language of the De Stijl (The Style) movement, which was launched in Europe in the second decade of the twentieth century by Dutch artists Piet Mondrian and Theo van Doesburg. Diller remained faithful to his own version of De Stijl until his death in 1965, believing throughout his life that abstract relationships could harbor universal truths. The quiet purity of his art seems to reflect the isolation he often felt in life. It was only with the rise of Minimalism in the 1960s that Diller gained legitimacy as the preeminent American of an earlier generation to work in a geometric style.

In the late 1920s, Diller studied at the Art Students League in New York, where he was a pupil of Hans Hofmann. In 1933, he saw reproductions of the work of Van Doesburg, whose writings led him, in turn, to the work of Mondrian. By the mid-1930s, Diller had brought his visual language within the limits of De Stijl: straight lines and rectangular planes in orthogonal arrangement, the three primary colors, and black and white.

Diller developed his work according to a set of three "themes," which he first described in a brochure for an exhibition at the Rose Fried Gallery in 1951 and later diagrammed in a chart for an exhibition at the Galerie Chalette in 1961. He thought of these themes as dialectical moments in a larger process rather than as strict categories. The first theme featured free-floating rectangles against a flat surface plane; the second consisted of isolated rectangles generated by continuous lines; and the third presented rectangles fully locked into a grid. At this last stage, the once-free element had been destroyed and the entire surface of the work was activated: planes and bands crisscrossed, confusing figure and ground. Taken together, the three themes demonstrate Diller's close attention to Mondrian's work. They suggest, respectively, Mondrian's 1917 paintings with free-floating color blocks; his classic Neoplastic works of the 1920s; and his last, exuberant Boogie-Woogie paintings, made in New York in the early 1940s.

In 1958, Diller returned to his First Theme series, which he had begun in the 1930s. *First Theme* (1964) is an example of the black-ground pictures that became Diller's primary focus during the last five years of his life. The square canvas measures 42 by 42 inches, a size and shape he favored. A yellow rectangular block touches the bottom edge of the canvas while blue and white forms hover on either side. Diller constantly experimented by mixing paints from different manufacturers until he achieved the right hue and consistency for a given work. "A primary color is a snare and a delusion. There isn't any such thing," he contended. "No one primary is absolute; they are conceived only in relation to one another."[1] He used a collage approach when planning his paintings, moving pieces of colored construction paper and holding them in place with pins to arrive at an arrangement that was intuitive, never calculated. Later, he made sure to eliminate the pinholes so as not to detract from his desired effect of a flat, matte, continuous surface. At times he even sanded shiny areas that he considered distracting.[2] He also added turpentine to paint to reduce gloss. In *First Theme*, the black paint has been rubbed with pumice.[3]

PR

---

[1] Burgoyne Diller, quoted in Elaine de Kooning, "Diller Paints a Picture," *ARTnews* 51, no. 9 (January 1953): 55.

[2] Ibid.

[3] Nina C. Sundell, ed., *The Robert and Jane Meyerhoff Collection: 1958–1979* (Baltimore: Baltimore Museum of Art, 1980), 17.

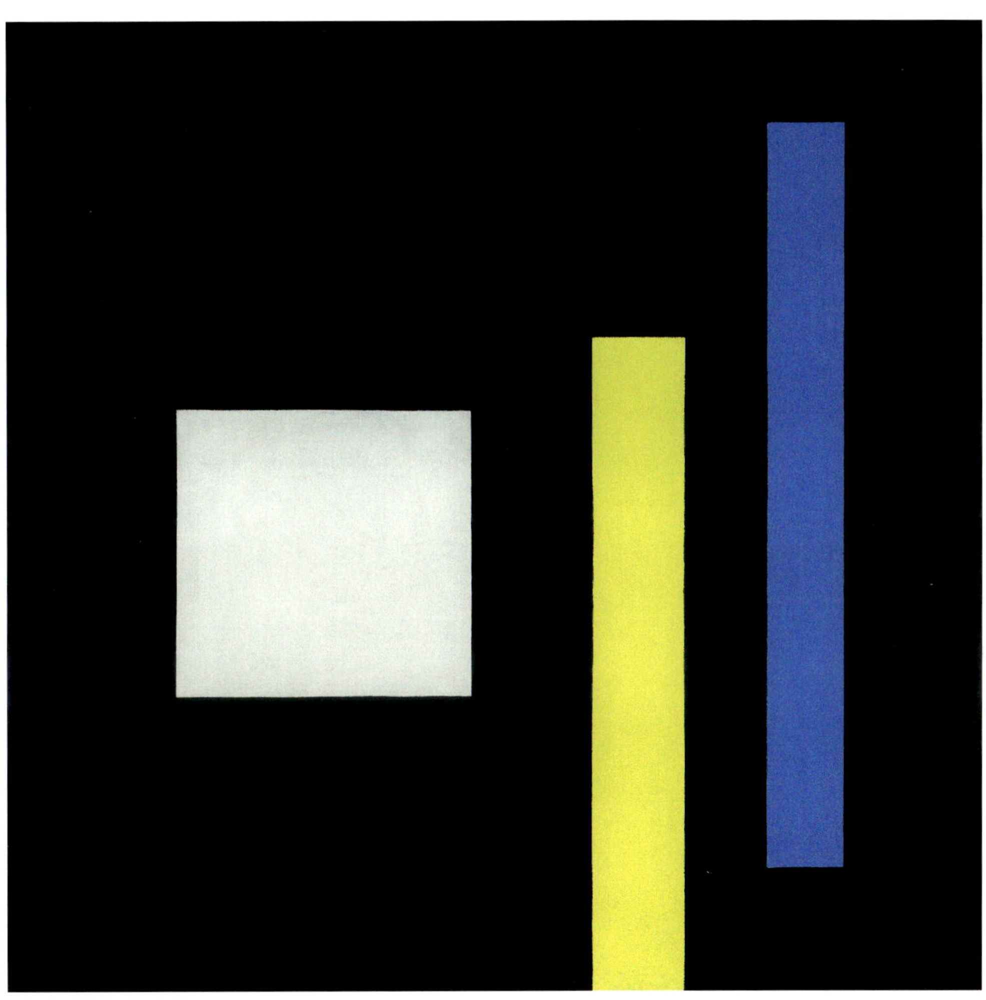

21. Burgoyne Diller, *First Theme*, 1964. Oil on canvas, 42 x 42 in. (106.7 x 106.7 cm). 1994.82.2

JEAN DUBUFFET

FRENCH, 1901–1985

Born in Le Havre, Jean Dubuffet moved to Paris in 1918 and studied painting briefly at the Académie Julian. In 1925, after several unsuccessful attempts to establish himself as an artist, he took over his father's wine business. He started painting again for a short period in the thirties, but it was not until 1942 that he began the work that made him famous. Dubuffet moved through more than twenty different self-proclaimed phases in the next four decades; the champion of disorder and.discovery classified his own production carefully.[1]

Dubuffet studied and collected the art of the untutored and mentally ill and emulated it in his own work. He coined the term *art brut* (rough or raw art), commenting: "It is my belief that only in this *art brut* can we find the natural and normal processes of artistic creation in their pure and elementary state."[2] His vibrantly colored paintings of the early 1940s gave way in the 1950s to crudely drawn, energetic images with deeply abraded surfaces made of materials such as sand, plaster, tar, gravel, and ashes bound with varnish and glue. In the mid-fifties Dubuffet was occupied almost exclusively by a series of collaged paintings made of cutout scraps of painted canvas.

Dubuffet returned to the assemblage technique in 1975 in a cycle of works called *Théâtres de mémoire* (Theaters of Memory); by August 1978, he had produced nearly one hundred of them. He completed *La ronde des images*, among the largest canvases in the group, on April 19, 1977. The *Théâtres de mémoire* were created from a combination of new paintings on paper made specifically for the series[3] and cut-up sections of the earlier *Lieux abrégés* series, which immediately preceded the *Théâtres*.[4] Dubuffet devised a painstaking method for the final realization of the *Théâtres*: when it became difficult to move the cutouts around on the floor, the artist affixed magnets to the back of the cutouts so he could move them around on the large metal sheets he had attached to his studio walls. Once he achieved a satisfactory arrangement through layering and reshuffling, Dubuffet made precise diagrams and took exact measurements. His assistant then glued the sheets to the canvas.[5]

After finishing several of the *Théâtres*, Dubuffet came up with the title of the series based on his reading of *The Art of Memory* (1966) by the Renaissance historian Frances A. Yates. Tracing the art of memory from the Greek orators to the seventeenth century, the book recounts how people learned to retain vast amounts of knowledge before the invention of the printed page.[6] Dubuffet may have been directly influenced by Yates's description of the "theater of memory" as conceived by the Italian philosopher Giulio Camillo in the sixteenth century: it was marked by "many images, and full of little boxes; there are various orders and grades in it," in which "each individual figure and ornament" is given a specific place.[7] Likewise, the rapidly drawn figures in *La ronde des images* seem to inhabit separate boxes within their discrete cutouts. Hubert Damisch argues that by linking the series with classical erudition, Dubuffet challenges narrow criticisms of *art brut* as merely a "battle against . . . Greco-Roman culture." Rather, the series entrenches the artist within this very tradition.[8]
KR

---

[1] Working deliberately in one series at a time, Dubuffet would release its products in a well-coordinated exhibition with an accompanying catalogue. The thirty-seven volumes of the catalogue raisonné (Paris, 1964–1984) owe much to the artist's own conscientiousness.

[2] Dubuffet, quoted in *Jean Dubuffet: Works, Writings, and Interviews*, éds. Valérie Da Costa and Fabrice Hergott (Barcelona: Ediciones Polígrafa, 2006), 11, originally quoted in *Prospectus et tous écrits suivants*, vol. 2 (Paris: Gallimard, 1967), 203–204.

[3] In 1976, Dubuffet told the dealer Arnold Glimcher that after completing nineteen assemblages, he planned to begin "painting components especially for the assemblages." He added that he felt that this approach would be "good for stimulating inventiveness; for each stage brings suggestions for the other." See Jean Dubuffet, excerpt from a letter to Arnold Glimcher, April 27, 1976, published in *Jean Dubuffet: Les dernières années* (Paris: Jeu de Paume, 1991), 283–284.

[4] Mildred Glimcher, *Jean Dubuffet: Towards an Alternative Reality* (New York: Pace Publications, Inc., 1987), 19.

[5] A few of the artist's diagrams for the *Théâtres de mémoire* series are reproduced in *Jean Dubuffet: Les dernières années*, 90; *Jean Dubuffet: Recent Work, 1974–1976*, exh. cat. (New York: Pace Gallery, 1976); and Glimcher, *Jean Dubuffet*, 24.

[6] See Frances A. Yates, *The Art of Memory* (Chicago: University of Chicago Press, 1966).

[7] Ibid., 136.

[8] Hubert Damisch, "*Théâtres de Mémoire*: After-Effects," published in English in *Jean Dubuffet: Les dernières années*, 282–284.

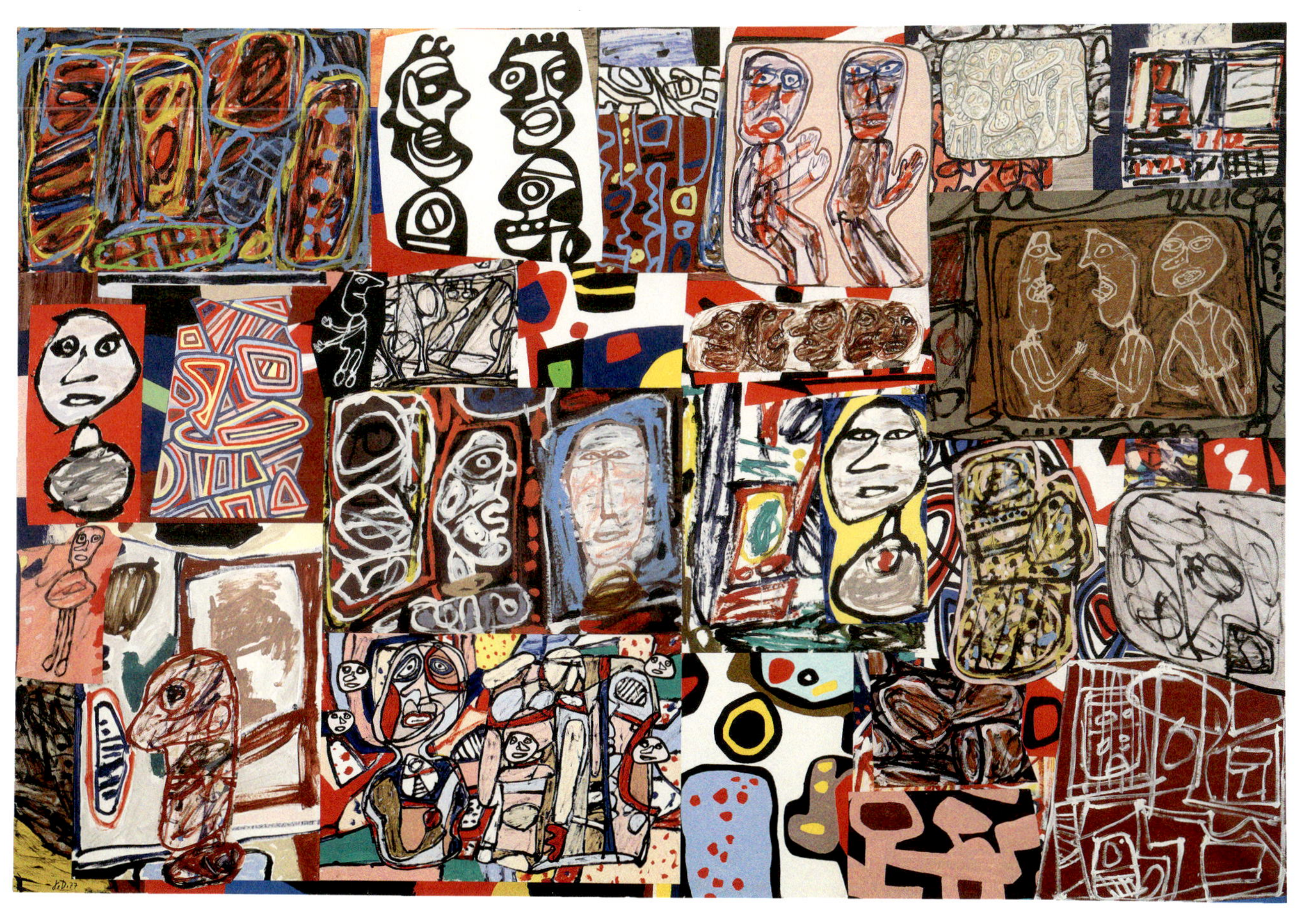

22. Jean Dubuffet, *La ronde des images*, 1977. Acrylic on paper on canvas, 98 x 142 in. (248.9 x 360.7 cm). 1996.81.5

ERIC FISCHL

AMERICAN, b. 1948

Born in New York City in 1948, Eric Fischl was raised on Long Island. He studied painting at the California Institute of the Arts and graduated in 1972. In 1974, Fischl began teaching at the Nova Scotia College of Art and Design in Halifax. He resigned his post after four years and returned to New York City, where he began to make paintings that imagined uncomfortably intimate, sexually charged moments in middle-class suburban settings.[1] Fischl was part of an international cohort of artists—German, American, French, Italian—who burst into art-world consciousness in the early 1980s and were soon lumped together as Neo-Expressionists. Rejecting the strictures of Minimalism and Conceptualism, these artists sought to reinvigorate painting by reviving elements from German Expressionism, Abstract Expressionism, and many other -isms. In a 1987 interview, Fischl explained that "the artists of my generation feel that you can borrow freely from any time and place to construct your own image. . . . In that sense I think I am a postmodernist."[2]

The multi-part, constructed format of *Saigon, Minnesota* derives in part from the artist's graphic work. From 1976 to 1982, Fischl created large works by drawing on sheets of transparent glassine with black oil paint and layering the sheets to create subtly disjunctive narratives. In the composite print *Year of the Drowned Dog* (1983), he turned from layering to juxtaposition in order to achieve an equal degree of complexity. The print is composed of six color etchings, which together depict eight people and a dead dog on a tropical beach. Each etching is a self-contained picture; the changes in lighting and shadow from panel to panel indicate that the scenes occur at different times of day.[3] This work was the model for the nearly twenty-five-foot-long, four-panel painting *Saigon, Minnesota*.[4]

In this and other multi-panel works, Fischl explored what he terms the "links between time and memory and between physical and psychological space."[5] In the multi-panel paintings, Fischl explains, "I wanted the viewer to see that for me, the act of discovery and the act of execution were simultaneous. I wanted the viewer to participate in the re-creation of a scene, piecing it together from fragments and impressions, almost like a crime scene."[6] Fischl would prepare several blank canvases prior to beginning these monumental works.[7] As the narrative of a given painting developed, he might add a new canvas in order to extend the picture plane, allowing the size and shape of the work to evolve organically.

The iconography in Fischl's art is deliberately ambiguous. According to the artist, the title for *Saigon, Minnesota* came to him as some of the figures took on an Asian American appearance while he painted. At the time, the national press was obsessively reporting on an alleged child-abuse scandal in a small Minnesota town. These two factors led Fischl to decide that the scene was located "somewhere between Saigon and Minnesota."[8] The juxtaposition of clothed and unclothed figures, children and adults of potentially disparate nationalities, and the presence of the one-armed man at center evoke associations with the Vietnam War as well as sexual abuse, but the enigmatic relationship among the figures makes it impossible to determine if anything transgressive is occurring.[9]

Art critic Peter Schjeldahl considers *Saigon, Minnesota* a transitional work in the artist's oeuvre, one which signals "a kind of Copernican shift, a displacement at the center of gravity from inside to outside the picture. The change is from scenario to tableau, from the personal to the social, and from obsession to ambivalence."[10]

KR

---

[1] For more on sociological and sexual overtones in Fischl's work, see Robert Storr, "Desperate Pleasures," *Art in America* 72, no. 10 (November 1984): 124–130; and Arthur C. Danto, Robert Enright, and Steve Martin, *Eric Fischl: 1970–2007* (New York: Monacelli Press, 2008).

[2] Eric Fischl, interview by Donald Kuspit, in *Fischl* (New York: Vintage, 1987), 33.

[3] Elizabeth Armstrong proposes that the viewer may reorder the individual sheets in *Year of the Drowned Dog* to suggest different narratives. However, it seems more likely that the sheets should be matched up according to their common horizon lines. Armstrong, "Eric Fischl's Monotypes: In the Continuum," in *Scenes and Sequences: Recent Monotypes by Eric Fischl* (Hanover, NH: Dartmouth College, 1990), 57.

[4] The direct relationship between *Year of the Drowned Dog* and *Saigon, Minnesota* is discussed in Peter Schjeldahl, *Eric Fischl* (New York: Art in America and Stewart, Tabori & Chang, 1988), 27; and Armstrong, "Eric Fischl's Monotypes," 58.

[5] Fischl, quoted in Eric Fischl with Michael Stone, *Bad Boy: My Life On and Off the Canvas* (New York: Crown Publishers, 2012), 200.

[6] Ibid.

[7] In 2012, Fischl stated that although he liked creating the multi-panel works, he abandoned the technique because the cantilevered canvases were "just too inelegant and clunky." Ibid.

[8] Schjeldahl, *Eric Fischl*, 27.

[9] Jeffrey Weiss, "Eric Fischl," in Mark Rosenthal, ed., *The Robert and Jane Meyerhoff Collection: 1945–1995*, exh. cat. (Washington, DC: National Gallery of Art, 1996), 50.

[10] Schjeldahl, *Eric Fischl*, 28.

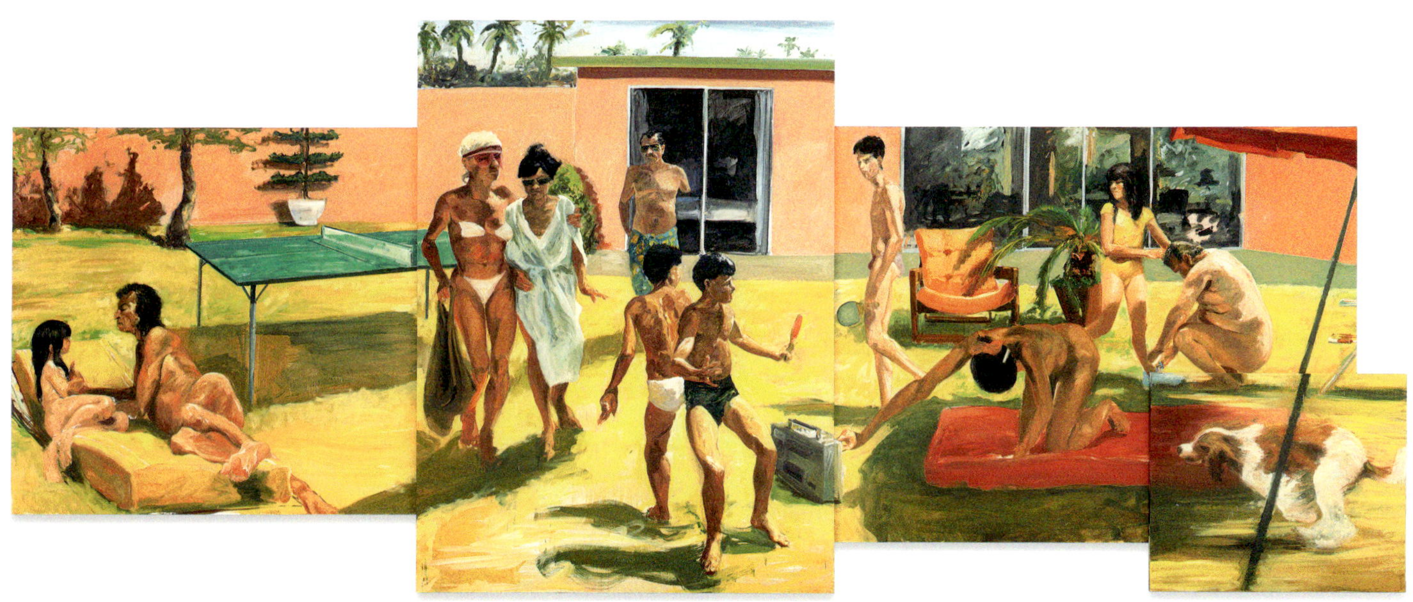

23. Eric Fischl, *Saigon, Minnesota*, 1985. Oil on canvas (four joined panels), overall: 120 x 296 1/8 in. (304.8 x 752 cm). 1992.28.7.1-4

NANCY GRAVES

AMERICAN, 1939–1995

Nancy Graves graduated from Vassar College in 1961 and earned an MFA from Yale University School of Art and Architecture in 1964. In 1969, she became the first woman to have a solo exhibition at the Whitney Museum of American Art. Graves was a filmmaker and world traveler who incorporated elements of classical antiquity as well as Egyptian, African, Japanese, Korean, and Indian art into her eclectic, exuberant work. She also mined the natural world for her imagery.

When Graves began her graduate studies at Yale in 1961, Josef Albers had just retired. The faculty and visiting artists were a diverse group that included William Bailey, Edwin Dickinson, Philip Guston, Alex Katz, Jack Tworkov, and Neil Welliver; no single manner of working was imposed on the students. Although Abstract Expressionism was still dominant, Graves painted small, colorful, Matisse-like still lifes. She found her own voice in the later 1960s with life-size sculptures of camels—constructions of wood, burlap, hair, and wax that seemed like funky versions of the animals in natural history displays. These works were rooted in her childhood memories of the animals preserved by taxidermists in the Berkshire Museum, where her father worked.

In 1971, Graves temporarily gave up sculpture to resume painting, and toward the end of the decade she became interested in archaeology. Awarded a residency at the American Academy in Rome in 1979, she used the opportunity to explore paleontology and cave painting, and to tour ancient excavation sites throughout the Mediterranean. These digs showed Graves how cultures become layered over time, each new civilization absorbing the previous one.

Painted in 1980 upon her return to New York, *Agualine* seems to capture this palimpsest of history in its complex layering and fragmenting of color, form, and line. The painting builds on a visual vocabulary that Graves developed through the 1970s, but pushes figurative references toward abstraction. The band of thickly applied orange brushstrokes across the lower right corner of the canvas recalls a type of carved bone or horn found at Upper Paleolithic sites. Compositionally, the work is reminiscent of an earlier painting, *Scaux* (1977), in which Graves used an opaque projection to transfer linear patterns from cave drawings and objects in Altamira, Spain.[1] In *Agualine*, the brown and black lines dancing across the canvas borrow from the same sources but are more loosely transcribed. *Agualine* also differs from the gray-toned *Scaux* in its high-keyed palette, foreshadowing the vibrant and colorful patinas Graves would use in her sculpture of the 1980s.

The title *Agualine* has a maritime connotation. A compound of the words *agua* (Spanish for "water") and "line," this invented term calls to mind ancient aqueducts or underwater life. The fluidity of the paint handling and the variety of marks suggest the tracks of creatures moving across the seafloor and recall Graves's paintings of the early 1970s, which were based on ocean-floor cartography.

KR

---

[1] See Thomas Padon, *Nancy Graves: Excavations in Print: A Catalogue Raisonné* (New York: Harry N. Abrams, Inc., 1996), 21. Though the title of *Scaux* refers in particular to the famous Lascaux caves in France, Graves drew on images from various Upper Paleolithic caves.

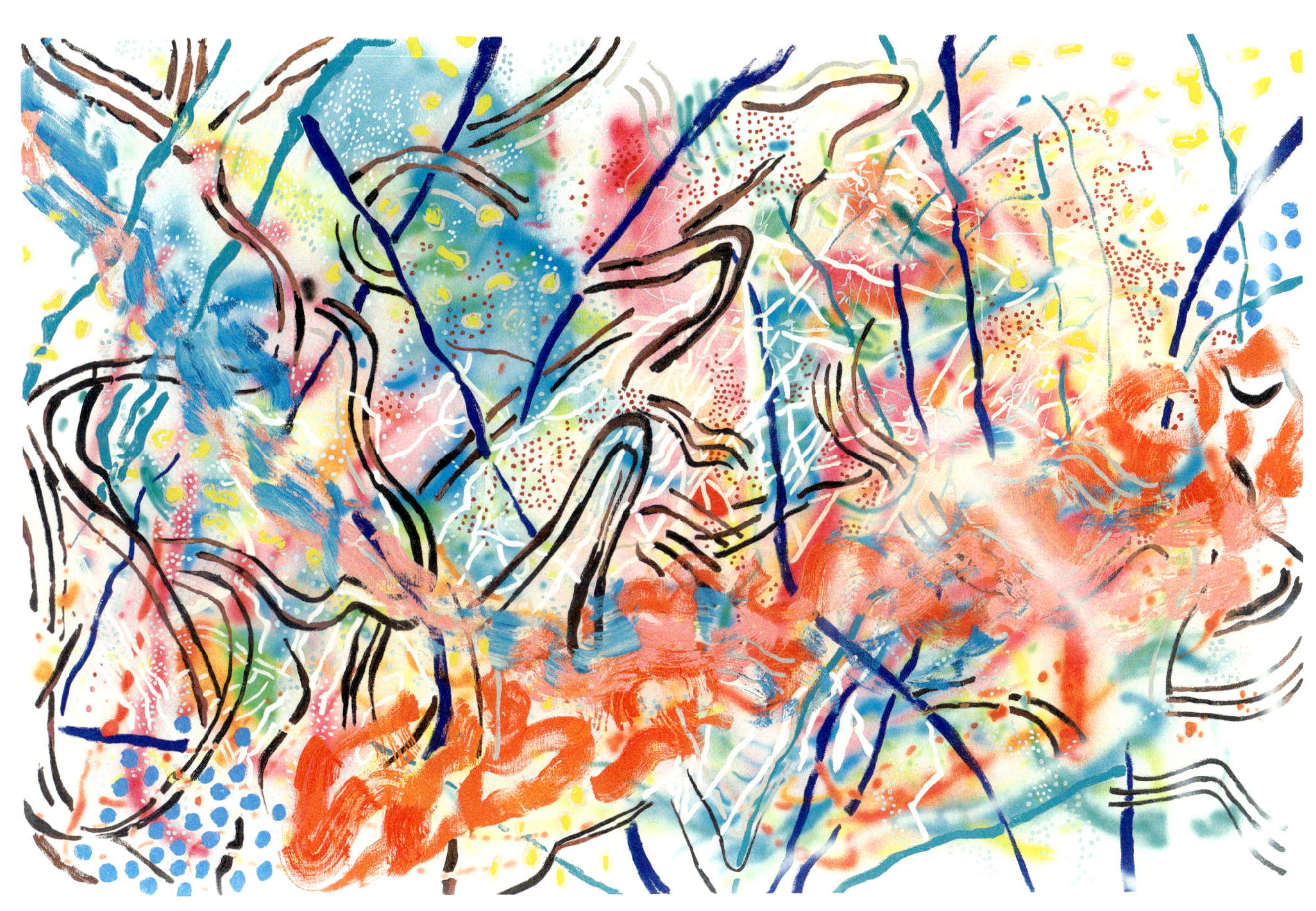

24. Nancy Graves, *Agualine*, 1980. Oil on canvas, 44 x 66 in. (111.8 x 167.6 cm). 2010.14.1

PHILIP GUSTON

AMERICAN, b. CANADA, 1913–1980

Critics and colleagues alike roundly condemned Philip Guston for his 1970 exhibition at New York's Marlborough Gallery, where *Courtroom* made its debut. The show, now legendary, marked Guston's return to figuration following a much-admired phase of painterly abstraction from 1950 to 1968. The Marlborough reviewers judged Guston guilty of retreating to the figurative style and political content of his art of the 1930s, and in particular to the Ku Klux Klan figures that had haunted his formative years. (Born Philip Goldstein in Montreal, Guston moved with his family in 1919 to Los Angeles, where the Klan was active.) That Guston brought back these images in a style that owed much to cartoonists such as George Herriman did not help matters: Hilton Kramer called Guston "a mandarin pretending to be a stumblebum," and Robert Hughes referred to his "Ku Klux Komix."[1] These readings missed the black humor of Guston's work, overlooked its virtuoso paint handling, and ignored the fact that figures had been lurking in his abstractions for years. Rather than replacing one style or subject with another, Guston had combined elements of his figurative and abstract vocabularies to create a new and important body of work.

While Guston was upset by this response to his work, he seems to have anticipated it at some level, for *Courtroom* both heralds the new manner and symbolically depicts its rebuke by the art establishment of the time. The horizontal composition divides roughly in two: the right side features a partly hidden clock, a small whitish painting or drawing, and a large black-sheathed arm with a red Mickey Mouse hand pointing an accusatory index finger. The wall behind is painted in the rosy hues and brushy manner of Guston's 1960s abstractions, suggesting that the accusation emanates from the perspective of his preceding work. On the left side in the foreground is one of Guston's "hoods" or "heads," as he called these clunky figures in their hand-stitched, pieced-together robes. The hood holds a cigar with his middle and index fingers (Guston was a smoker).[2] This figure, cut off at the waist by the bottom edge of the canvas, is an amalgam of wrong-doing Klansman and tortured artist; covered with patches of red paint or blood, he represents the artist caught literally red-handed by himself. Behind the hood is a trash can filled with nail-studded stretcher bars and another figure—head down, visible only from the legs up—representing the hood's or the artist's other half. In effect, we see Guston accusing, dividing, discarding, and remaking himself all at once.

The iconography of Guston's late work is intertwined with personal and art historical references. *Courtroom*'s title reflects the idea of self-adjudication in the practice of painting, a topic on which Guston reflected in 1966:

> The canvas is a court where the artist is prosecutor, defendant, jury and judge.
> Art without a trial disappears at a glance: it is primitive or hopeful, or mere notions, or merely startling, or just another means of making life bearable. You cannot settle out of court.[3]

Guston's hoods recall not only Klansmen, but also the hooded flagellants often depicted in the Quattrocento paintings that he loved. The pointing hand and the metaphor of creation in *Courtroom* evoke Michelangelo's "Creation of Adam" (1511–1512), while the inverted figure and the references to good and evil recall another of his masterpieces in the Sistine Chapel, the *Last Judgment* (1536–1541).[4] In this light, the legs in the trash may make particular reference to the allegorical figure of Avarice, free-falling into hell. Like *Courtroom*, Michelangelo's fresco is widely believed to incorporate a self-portrait of the artist, hidden in the flayed skin of Saint Bartholomew. (One commentator locates a hidden self-portrait in *Courtroom* in the green blob just below the pointing finger.)[5] Considered a pivotal masterpiece that helped to inaugurate the wild creativity of Guston's last decade, *Courtroom* shares the same fate as Michelangelo's *Last Judgment*, which was criticized in its own day (for its inclusion of nude figures) only to be redeemed in time and judged a masterpiece.

MD

---

1 Hilton Kramer, "A Mandarin Pretending to Be a Stumblebum," *New York Times*, October 25, 1970; and Robert Hughes, "Art: Ku Klux Komix," *Time*, November 9, 1970.

2 The work widely accepted as the key to Guston's self-portrait as a hooded figure is *The Studio* (1969), which features the hooded figure at an easel painting a hooded figure on canvas.

3 Philip Guston, "Faith, Hope, and Impossibility," *ARTnews Annual* 31 (1966):103.

4 Donald Kuspit has also referenced the connection to Michelangelo's "Creation of Adam" in "Philip Guston's Self-Doubt," Artnet.com, www.artnet.com/magazine/features/kuspit/kuspit12-4-03.asp., accessed February 24, 2014.

5 See Robert Slifkin, *Out of Time: Philip Guston and the Refiguration of Postwar American Art* (Berkeley and Los Angeles: University of California Press, 2013), 124.

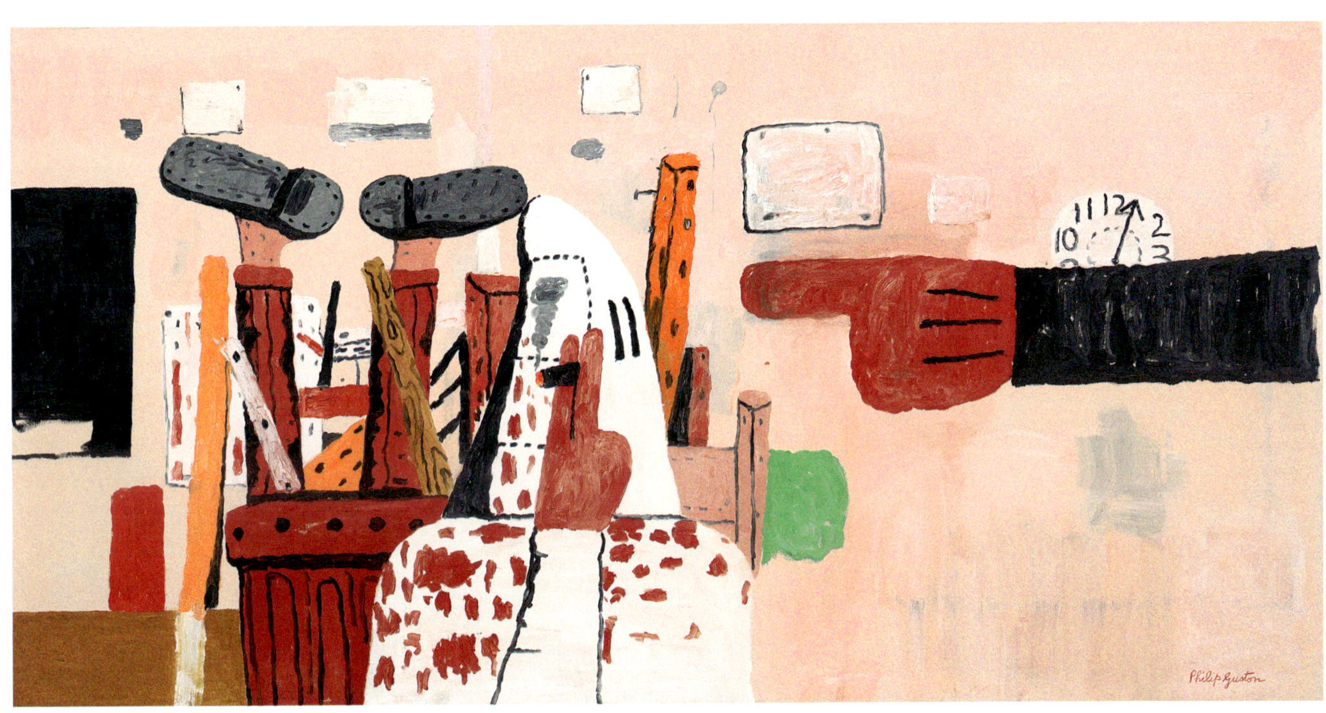

25. Philip Guston, *Courtroom*, 1970. Oil on canvas, 67 x 129 in. (170.2 x 327.7 cm). Collection of Robert and Jane Meyerhoff

GRACE HARTIGAN

AMERICAN, 1922–2008

Grace Hartigan survived the raucous heyday of Abstract Expressionism to become a dedicated teacher and painter renowned for her ability to combine abstraction and figuration into expressive wholes. In the late 1940s, Hartigan became friends with both Willem de Kooning and Jackson Pollock, and she soon adopted their allover composition, large scale, vivid color, expressive paint handling, and penchant for incorporating figurative references into abstract work. Perhaps the most significant lesson she drew from these friendships was an ideal of total commitment to art. As Hartigan proclaimed after meeting Pollock, "I knew the paintings and the person who painted them were one-and-the-same. Painting was not an activity but a total life. And you would do anything to keep painting, even if you starved. You were the paintings and the paintings were you."[1] The equation of self-expression and creation became her dogma. As she suggested in one interview, "The time I know when a painting is finished is when it leaves me alone. . . . When it finally does, I wouldn't dream of touching it. I get pregnant from the image I'm working on. I live with it, dream of it, and finally the labor pains begin."[2]

By 1953, Hartigan was a major figure in the milieu of second-generation New York School artists and had already received three solo exhibitions. She became close to the poet and art critic Frank O'Hara, collaborating with him in 1952 and 1953 on a dozen paintings that included handwritten texts of his poems. By the mid-1950s, Hartigan had begun her City Life series, which depicted advertising images, billboards, and shopwindows with radiant colors and active brushstrokes. With her move to Long Island, where she lived from 1957 to 1959, the Place paintings emerged, featuring abstracted landscapes that projected an intimacy with nature.

Essex and Hester (Red) occupies a privileged position between these two series. It recalls the bustling life of New York while incorporating the more abstract, lyrical character of the countryside. The painting is named for the intersection of Essex and Hester streets on the Lower East Side, near where she had lived before moving to the country. With its dominant expanse of deep red and its cursive strokes of black, the work captures the unruly rhythms of an urban landscape. The picture plane is declared by patches of color and by active brushwork full of movement and vibration. Black strokes annex small expanses, creating loosely defined shapes that may include a convertible automobile moving out of the picture at left.

But such references are fleeting, for Hartigan was after feel, not detail. "I have found my 'subject,'" she reflected in 1956, "[and] it concerns that which is vulgar and vital in American modern life, and the possibilities of its transcendence into the beautiful. I do not wish to *describe* my subject matter, or to reflect upon it—I want to distill it until I have its essence. Then the rawness must be resolved into form and unity; without the 'rage for order' how can there be art?"[3]

[1] Hartigan, quoted in Robert Saltonstall Mattison, *Grace Hartigan: A Painter's World* (New York: Hudson Hills Press, 1990), 12.

[2] James Thrall Soby, "An Interview with Grace Hartigan," *Saturday Review*, October 5, 1957, 26.

[3] Hartigan, quoted in Dorothy C. Miller, *12 Americans*, exh. cat. (New York: Museum of Modern Art, 1956), 53.

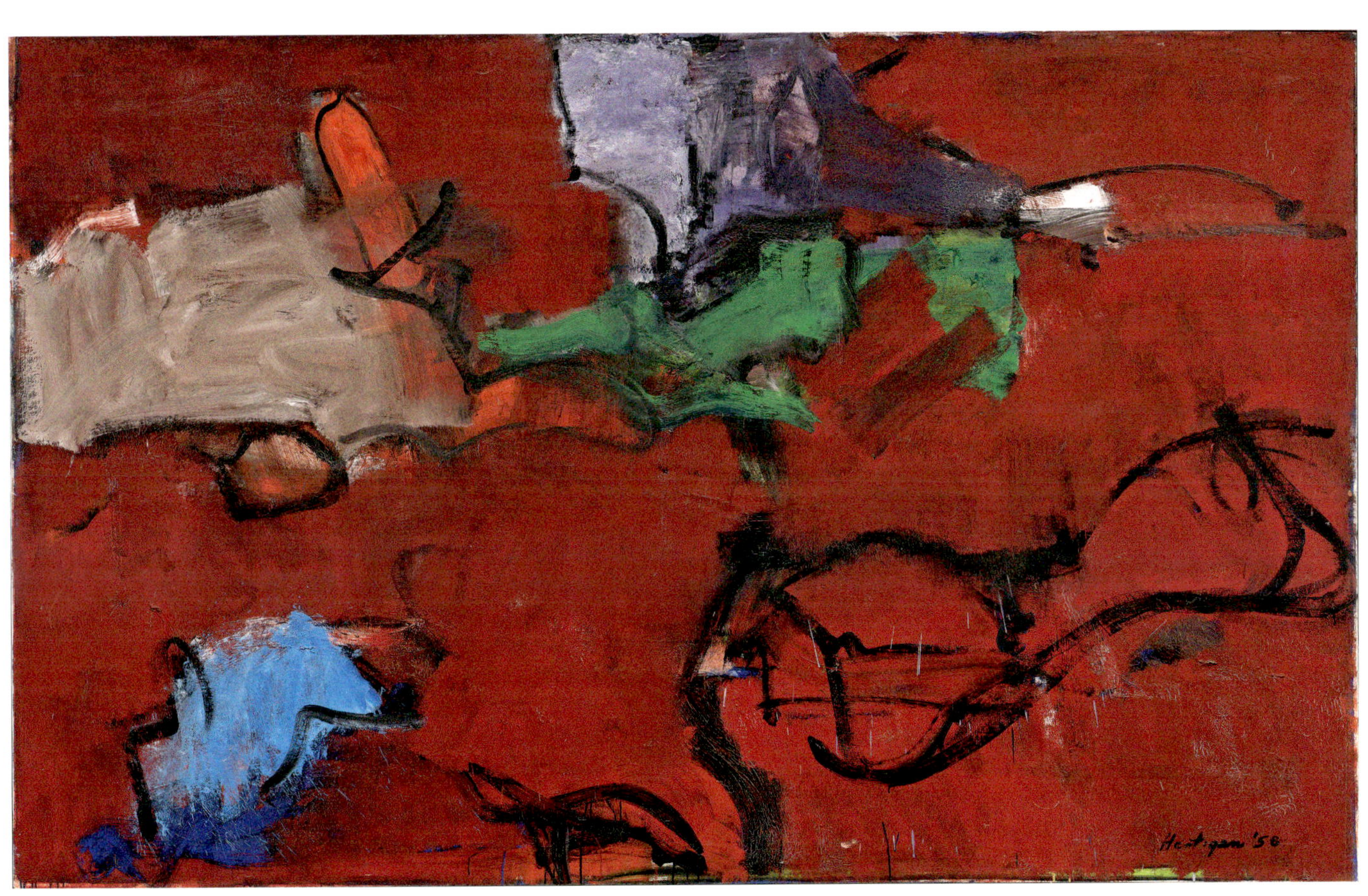

26. Grace Hartigan, *Essex and Hester (Red)*, 1958. Oil on canvas, 53 x 83 1/4 in. (134.6 x 211.5 cm). 1996.81.3

HOWARD HODGKIN

BRITISH, b. 1932

In 1984, Howard Hodgkin represented the United Kingdom at the Venice Biennale, securing his reputation as a major contemporary painter. The exhibition in the British Pavilion, which presented twenty-four of his works on walls painted pale green, underscored a turn in Hodgkin's art that had become increasingly apparent since the late 1970s.[1] It was then that he left behind hard edges and striped patterns for a seemingly improvisational technique of individual marks—drags of the brush, often containing several strands of color; blobs and splotches; and the occasional swirl or arrow. At Venice, the flat interlocking shapes and impacted interiors of Hodgkin's previous works dissolved into translucent washes of pigment and open, breathy spaces.

Much has been said about this change in his oeuvre, beginning with comments by his friend Bruce Chatwin, who made a coy allusion to a "chance encounter" that had allegedly introduced a "new kind of subject, and a new mood" to Hodgkin's art.[2] However, Hodgkin himself insisted that the content of his work and his process had remained essentially the same. It was at Venice, too, that Hodgkin became celebrated as a painter of small works or "cabinet pictures," paintings that do not clamor for attention but reveal themselves quietly and occupy little space.[3]

One work in the British Pavilion was definitely not small. *Souvenirs*, composed of two tightly joined panels together measuring 5 by 9 feet, was one of the largest paintings Hodgkin had yet made. In a conversation with the painter Patrick Caulfield, Hodgkin lamented the "terrible trouble" he had had completing the work. The problem was not just size, but a "multiple viewpoint" and a disjunction (Caulfield suggested) between its interior subject and its horizontal shape, which was better suited to landscape.[4] Indeed, Hodgkin has shown in a series of arresting abstract landscapes that a horizontal ground establishes an idea of a horizon; but he had long depicted interiors on horizontal grounds as well. For example, the first work he ever exhibited, *114 Sinclair Road* (1957–1958), is a representation of the artist's studio. It explores a multiple viewpoint in its attempt to capture the mood of the studio and the personalities of the five individuals gathered there.

The ambition of *Souvenirs* may be no different: a depiction, perhaps, of yet another apartment and a group of friends, it explores the sort of spatial and psychological ambiguity essayed in the prophetic early picture. A souvenir is both a memory and something that reminds us of a person, place, or event. *Souvenirs* is, to be sure, a wall of memory. As the title suggests, it contains not one reminiscence but several: note the configuration of white marks in the middle of the image, the rainbow at bottom left, the black arrow at far left, the gunmetal-gray swirl at far right, and other marks scattered throughout the image. Evocations of bodies and things and private exchanges, these shapes and daubs are veiled by a nearly allover pattern of large green blobs that functions as a foreground screen. Like any allover pattern, it keeps our vision dispersed and our focus mobile: we scan up and down the rows, only to settle temporarily on those marks (the rainbow, arrow, swirl, and so on) that interrupt the pattern.

And yet the word *allover* does not quite fit the painting. Unlike Frank Stella, who explored stripe patterns contemporaneously with the English painter, Hodgkin resists the allover grid, that durable convention of modernist art.[5] The pattern in *Souvenirs* is irregular, off. The rows of splotches (up to eleven high and twenty wide) lilt left and right.

Souvenirs is challenging to see: determined as we are to stand several feet away to perceive the total image, our efforts are repelled. We are instead drawn *toward*, almost *into*, Hodgkin's composition in order to peer closely, even microscopically, at its variegated surfaces and marks, abstract evocations of remembered feelings. And in these acts of looking, other layers of brushwork and other marks are slowly revealed.

JM

---

1 As noted by Teresa Gleadowe in *Howard Hodgkin: Forty Paintings, 1977–84*, exh. cat. (London: Whitechapel Art Gallery, 1984), n.p.

2 Bruce Chatwin, "A Portrait of the Artist," in *Howard Hodgkin: Indian Leaves* (London and New York: Petersburg Ltd., 1982), 17. The encounter in question was sexual. (Hodgkin came out as a gay man during the late 1970s.) For a reading that emphasizes painterly gesture and phenomenology of touch more than biography in the evolution of Hodgkin's style, see James Meyer, "Hodgkin's Body," in *Howard Hodgkin*, ed. Nicholas Serota (London: Tate Publishing, 2006).

3 To many visitors, Hodgkin's installation offered a welcome antidote to then-prevalent Neo-Expressionism: the large, portentous canvases of Anselm Kiefer, the crockery-covered reliefs of Julian Schnabel, and the like. See Robert Hughes, "Gliding Over a Dying Reef," *Time*, July 2, 1984, 76–77.

4 "Howard Hodgkin and Patrick Caulfield in Conversation," *Art Monthly* 78 (July/August 1984): 4.

5 In *Dancing* (1959) and *Girl in a Museum* (1958–1960), the patterns of repeated green and black stripes are irregular. Figures step through these webs, disrupting their systematic nature.

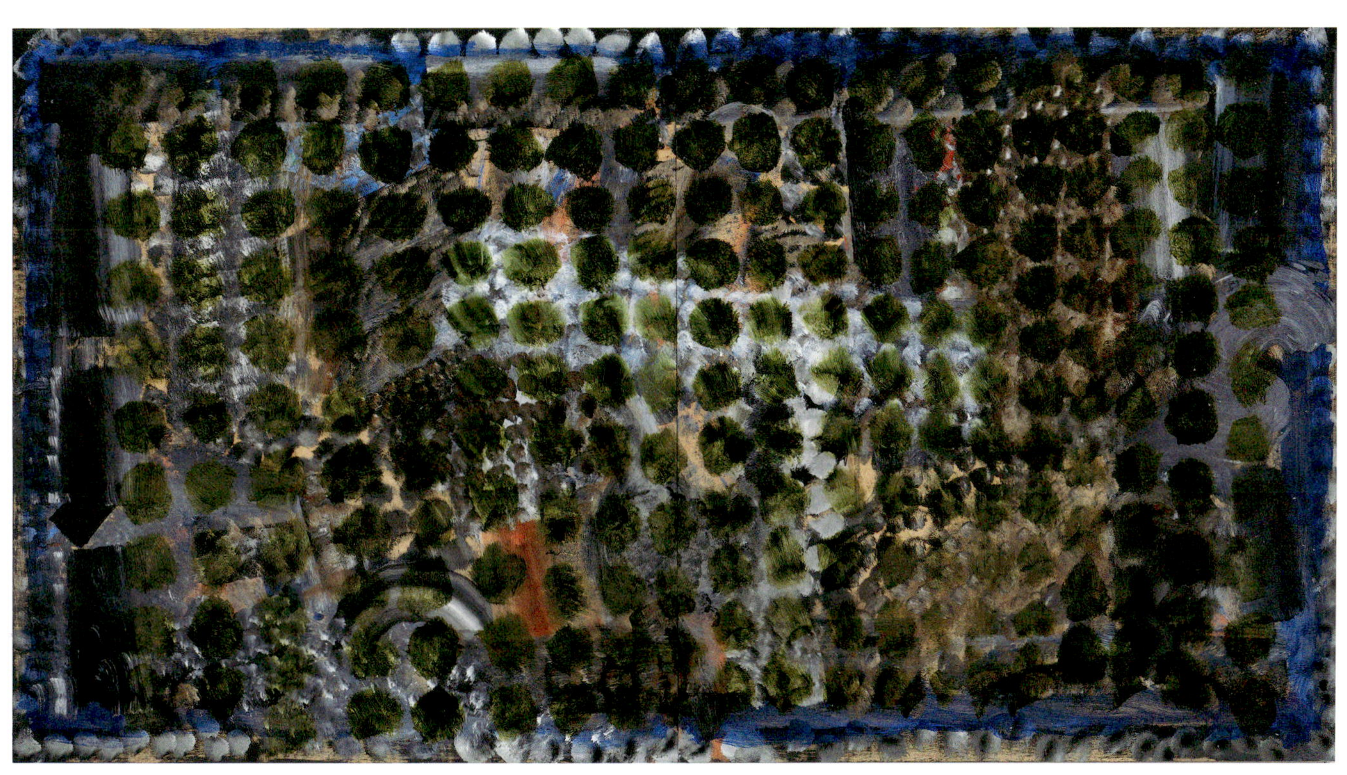

27. Howard Hodgkin, *Souvenirs*, 1980–1984. Oil on wood (two joined panels), overall: 60 x 108 in. (152.4 x 274.3 cm). 1994.82.3

HANS HOFMANN

AMERICAN, b. GERMANY, 1880–1966

Celebrated for his exuberant, color-filled canvases, Hans Hofmann played a pivotal role in the development of Abstract Expressionism. Born in Bavaria, he spent the decade before World War I in France, studying at the Académie Colarossi and the Académie de la Grande Chaumière and mingling with the Parisian avant-garde. He became especially friendly with the painter Robert Delaunay, whose writings on color and light informed Hofmann's own theories.[1] Nearly all of Hofmann's paintings from the Paris years were destroyed during the war. Hofmann was visiting Germany when war was declared, and was unable to return to France. Excused from service for medical reasons, he founded his own art school in Munich in 1915 in order to support himself. In a radical synthesis, Hofmann's pedagogical approach combined life studies with the teaching of more abstract and theoretical principles.[2]

Hofmann came to the United States in the summers of 1930 and 1931 to teach at the University of California at Berkeley, and moved to New York in 1934. Teaching in the city and (during the summers) in Provincetown, Massachusetts, he became "the most important art teacher of our time"[3] and "a major fountainhead of style and ideas for the 'new' American painting."[4]

Autumn Gold is an early example of Hofmann's best-known type of painting: works characterized by floating rectangular slabs of highly saturated color, rendered in thick impasto and aligned with the edges of the canvas. (These rectangles seem to have developed from the smaller dabs that Hofmann had used in previous works.)[5] The artist characterized the dynamic interaction of form, color, and material in his classic works as "push and pull."[6] His goal, explained in numerous teaching notes, was "plasticity," which he defined as "the transference of three-dimensional experience to two dimensions."[7] Each force was answered by a counterforce; each area of color produced a perceived change in every other area.

The picture plane in *Autumn Gold* is pulled apart by warm hues that seem to advance and cool hues that seem to retreat, even while it is restored by the materiality of colors and textures throughout the canvas. The deep purples, blues, and ochers are weighty; the pistachio greens and whitened yellows seem to levitate. For Hofmann, the result was a pictorial field "alive, dynamic, fluctuating and ambiguously dominated by forces and counter-forces, by movement and counter-movement, all of which summarize into rhythm and counter-rhythm as the quintessence of life experience."[8]

KR

---

[1] Conversely, Hofmann may have influenced Delaunay by drawing his attention to the color theories of Georges Seurat. See Helmut Friedel and Tina Dickey, *Hans Hofmann* (New York: Hudson Hills Press, 1997), 8; and Cynthia Goodman, "Hans Hofmann: A Master in Search of the 'Real,'" in *Hans Hofmann*, exh. cat. (New York: Whitney Museum of American Art in association with Prestel Verlag, 1990), 15.

[2] For an overview of Hofmann's teaching, see "Excerpts from the Teaching of Hans Hofmann," in *Search for the Real and Other Essays*, eds. Sara T. Weeks and Bartlett H. Hayes Jr., rev. ed. (Cambridge, MA: MIT Press, 1967).

[3] Clement Greenberg, "Art," *The Nation* (April 21, 1945): 469.

[4] Clement Greenberg, "Hans Hofmann: Grand Old Rebel," originally published in *ARTnews* (January 1959), repr. in *Clement Greenberg: The Collected Essays and Criticism*, vol. 4, *Modernism with a Vengeance, 1957–1969*, ed. John O'Brian (Chicago and London: University of Chicago Press, 1993), 67.

[5] Walter Darby Bannard, *Hans Hofmann: A Retrospective Exhibition*, exh. cat. (Washington, DC: Hirshhorn Museum and Sculpture Garden, 1976), 18.

[6] Hans Hofmann, "The Resurrection of the Plastic Arts," originally published in the catalogue for Hofmann's 1954 exhibition at the Samuel M. Kootz Gallery in New York; repr. in Sam Hunter, *Hans Hofmann* (New York: Harry N. Abrams, 1963), 44.

[7] Hans Hofmann, "Terms," in *Search for the Real and Other Essays*, 72.

[8] Hofmann, "The Resurrection of the Plastic Arts," 44.

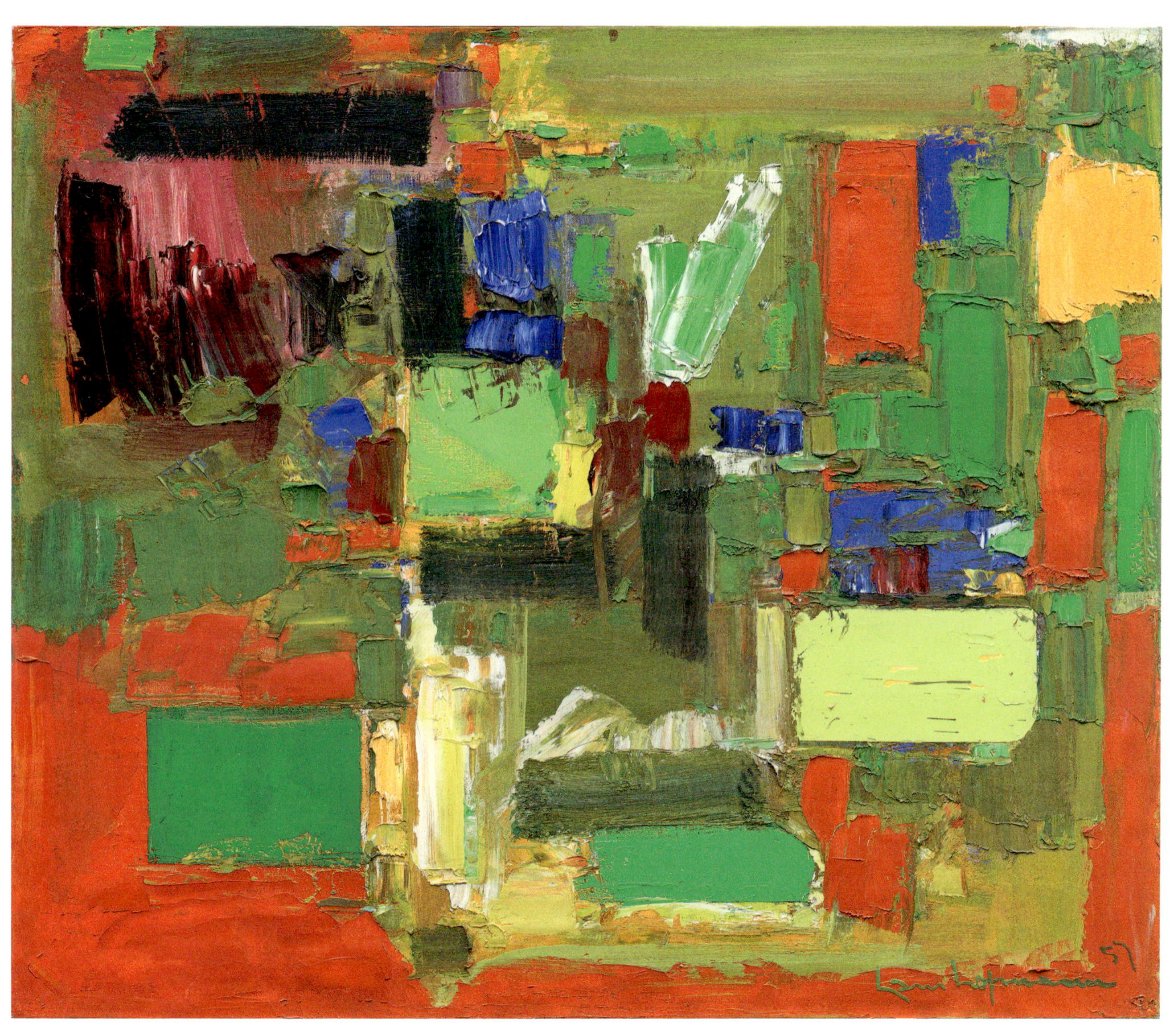

28. Hans Hofmann, *Autumn Gold*, 1957. Oil on canvas, 52 1/4 x 60 3/8 in. (132.7 x 153.4 cm). 1996.81.4

JASPER JOHNS

AMERICAN, b. 1930

Born in Georgia and raised in South Carolina, Jasper Johns started drawing at a young age, but lacked exposure to art or artists. He completed three semesters at the University of South Carolina before moving to New York, where he studied for two semesters at the Parsons School of Design, beginning in 1949. After a stint in the Army, he returned to New York and met Robert Rauschenberg, who was his romantic and artistic partner until 1961. Other important early associates and collaborators included the composer John Cage and the choreographer Merce Cunningham.

A painter, printmaker, draftsman, and sculptor, Johns is best known for the American flags and targets that he painted in 1954 and 1955, using encaustic (heated beeswax mixed with oil paint) and newspaper collage. Bold yet deadpan, energetic yet ordinary, these works caused a sensation in New York when Johns had his first solo exhibition there in 1958. At the time, the personal gestures and lofty claims of Abstract Expressionism still dominated the contemporary art scene. In such a context, Johns's choice of flat, recognizable subjects, so common as to be overlooked, was bracing. He was soon labeled a Neo-Dadaist, and, indeed, like Dada pioneer Marcel Duchamp (whom he came to know and admire), Johns freely blurred distinctions between painting and sculpture, fine and commercial art, art and object, and art and life.

With *Perilous Night*, we encounter the artist at a high point in his career, looking back to many of the devices that he had developed in prior decades, including the use of encaustic, the attachment of objects to the canvas, and the layering of references to his own and other artists' work. Much of the painting is dominated, although not obviously, by a reference to an Old Master source that Johns visited in person and reused many times, a detail from the Resurrection panel of Matthias Grünewald's *Isenheim Altarpiece* (1512–1516). The gray rectangular design at center right is based on Johns's tracing of a detail from a reproduction of the altarpiece, the two Roman soldiers at Christ's tomb. This is its first appearance in Johns's work. The same detail, reversed, rotated, and rendered with slightly more color, fills the left half of the painting. "I thought how moving it would be to extract the abstract quality of the work, its patterning, from the figurative meaning," Johns commented, yet "I could not get rid of the figure."[1]

Other art historical references abound: the nails with cast shadows and the wood graining reference Georges Braque's Cubist paintings of 1910, while the overall illusion of objects and images hanging on a wall recalls nineteenth-century trompe l'oeil still lifes. The spiky gray shape outlined in white at lower center may derive from the handkerchief depicted in Pablo Picasso's etching *Weeping Woman* (1937).[2] It also resembles the headgear of Grünewald's soldiers. There are various allusions to representations of the Crucifixion: a shroud, wooden boards, nails, and blood.

In addition to references and allusions, the painting includes real, or not so real, objects. Three ghoulish, bleeding cast-wax forearms, painted with something like Johns's signature flagstone pattern, hang from hooks. The artist made these casts from his model (a friend's son) at three-year intervals; they "grow" and "age" from left to right. Each arm drips a different color of blood: red, yellow, or blue, Johns's beloved primaries. Under the blue arm, he employed silkscreen to carefully reproduce manuscript pages from *The Perilous Night*, a Cage composition from 1943–1944. Cropping its pages, Johns amends the work of a composer known for his abrupt edits and silences. The punning at the edge is both amusing and significant: The "John" of Cage's name floats high above the artist's signature, "J. Johns," stenciled at lower right. The names are visually connected by an attached wooden slat, recalling the rotating devices that Johns often included in his work twenty years earlier. The same slat hides the "us" (the viewers?) in the word "perilous." Perhaps this uneasily dangling slat is there to remind us that any search for stable meaning and specific reference within Johns's work is indeed a perilous game.

JR

---

1 Jasper Johns, quoted in Richard Cork, "The Liberated Millionaire Is Not Flagging," *Times* (London), November 30, 1990, 21, repr. in *Jasper Johns: Interviews and Writings*, eds. Kirk Varnedoe and Christel Hollevoet (New York: Harry N. Abrams, 1996), 258.

2 Riva Castleman, *Jasper Johns: A Print Retrospective*, exh. cat. (New York: Museum of Modern Art, 1986), 45.

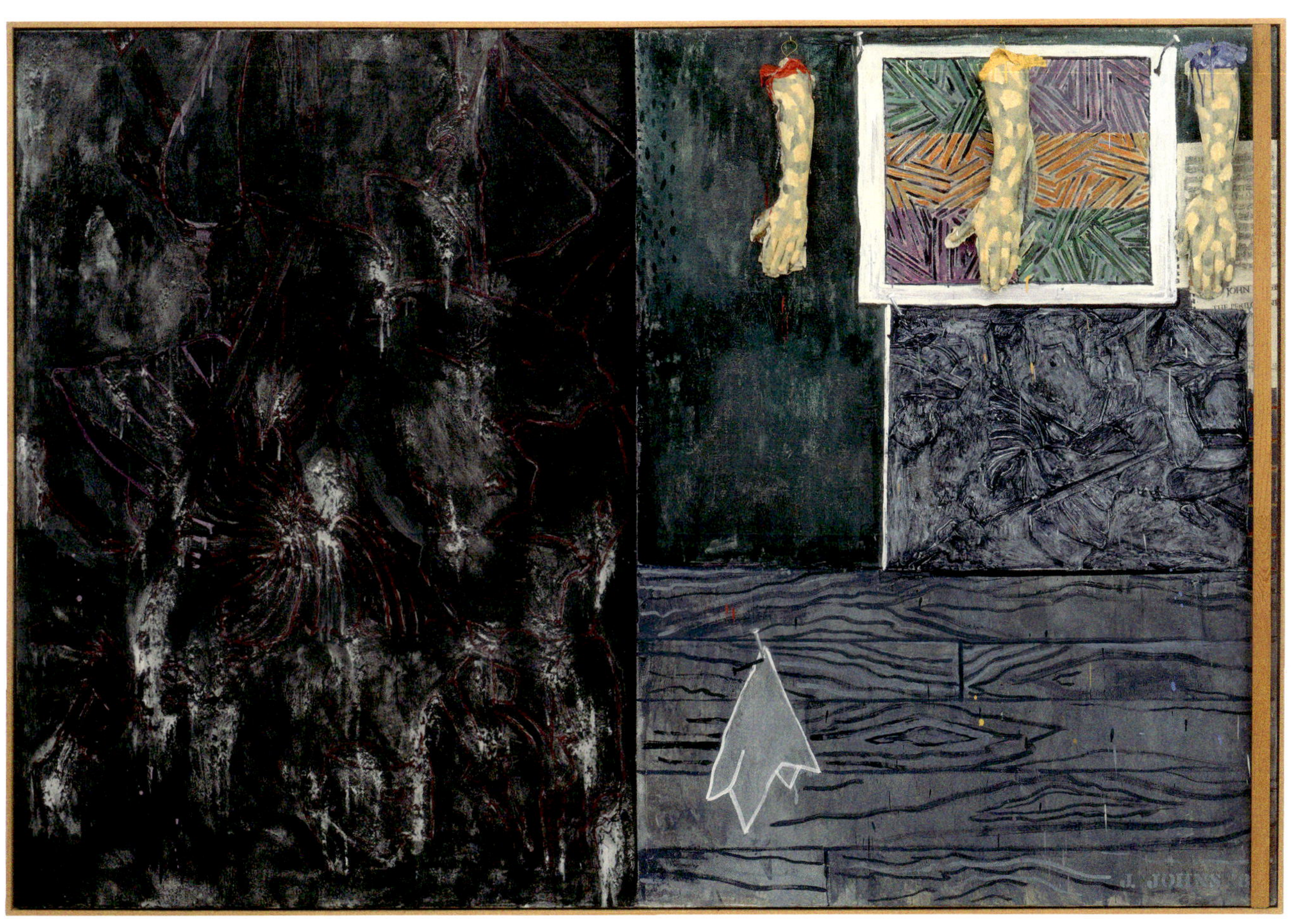

29. Jasper Johns, *Perilous Night*, 1982. Encaustic and silkscreen on canvas with objects, overall: 68 3/8 x 97 3/8 in. (173.5 x 247.2 cm). 1995.79.1

ELLSWORTH KELLY

AMERICAN, b. 1923

Since the late 1940s, Ellsworth Kelly has created paintings, sculptures, collages, prints, and drawings whose ceaseless exploration of shape, line, and color has been vital to the evolution of postwar modernism. He first gained critical recognition in the mid-1950s, when the Whitney Museum of American Art purchased his work and the Betty Parsons Gallery presented his first American solo exhibition. From the 1970s to the present day, the scale of Kelly's work has increased. He continues to join canvases of different sizes and shapes into asymmetrical formats and creates sculptures in bronze, wood, and steel. His visual vocabulary is drawn from observation of the world around him—shapes and colors found in plants and buildings, shadows on stairs, reflections on water—but is reshaped by his interest in the spaces between places and objects, and between his work and its viewers. Extracting motifs from context, Kelly translates and distills them to arrive at independent, self-contained works of art.

In the fall of 1964, Kelly created a series of collages that formed the basis for five lithographs in the November 1964 issue of the Galerie Maeght journal *Derrière le miroir*. One of these, printed in orange and green, is the clear predecessor of *Orange Green*.[1] The ovoid in the lithograph touches the bottom and left edges of the page but leaves a slight border at right, perhaps simply a result of an imperfection in assembling the magazine. Two years later, Kelly enlarged the print to create the Meyerhoff canvas, taking care to eliminate that right-hand border with its slight asymmetry. This concern with an odd detail that might otherwise escape notice is typical of Kelly. Another example of this is the painting's composition: despite the apparently strong half-and-half composition of the work, the orange form actually extends above the midline. Again and again, Kelly forces us to look twice before we trust our eyes. Just where we might expect classic balance, we find an unexpected twist.

Orange Green was made at a time when Kelly was especially preoccupied with the tensions and contradictions between forms and their backgrounds. While it is easy to read the orange shape as floating on a sea of green, the fact that the shape touches the edge on three sides facilitates a secondary reading of the green shape as three distinct shapes locking the orange into place; the similar value and intensity of the two colors also promote this reading. A different tension is created between Kelly's utterly flat handling of paint and the sense of space in the image, whether we see the orange in front of the green or even imagine that its surface swells out toward us, as its curving edge suggests.

Orange Green reflects Kelly's long-standing interest in the phenomenology of vision, the manner in which we see. His love of frontality, sharp edges, singular forms, saturated colors, and anonymous surfaces seems designed to bring the issue into sharp focus. The artist has said, "Most people don't learn how to see. They 'think' what they see. I try to separate the mind, and to see with the mind at rest."[2] Clearly Kelly delights in this challenge: "The most pleasurable thing in the world, for me, is to *see something*, and then translate how I see it."[3]

KR

---

[1] Kelly was the subject of three issues of the journal *Derrière le miroir*, produced and published by the Galerie Maeght in Paris. The journal was devoted exclusively to contemporary art and was published six times annually. Individual issues served as catalogues for Maeght exhibitions. See Richard H. Axsom, *The Prints of Ellsworth Kelly: A Catalogue Raisonné 1949–1985* (New York: Hudson Hills Press in association with the American Federation of Arts, 1987), 174–179. The lithograph is reproduced on page 178 of the catalogue raisonné. It was originally published in *Derrière le miroir* 149 (November 1964): 6.

[2] Ellsworth Kelly, interview with Robert Saltonstall Mattison, February 29, 1994, quoted in Mattison, "Ellsworth Kelly," in *Masterworks in the Robert and Jane Meyerhoff Collection* (New York: Hudson Hills Press, 1995), 141.

[3] Kelly, quoted in Elizabeth C. Baker, *Ellsworth Kelly: Recent Paintings and Sculptures*, exh. cat. (New York: Metropolitan Museum of Art, 1979), 7.

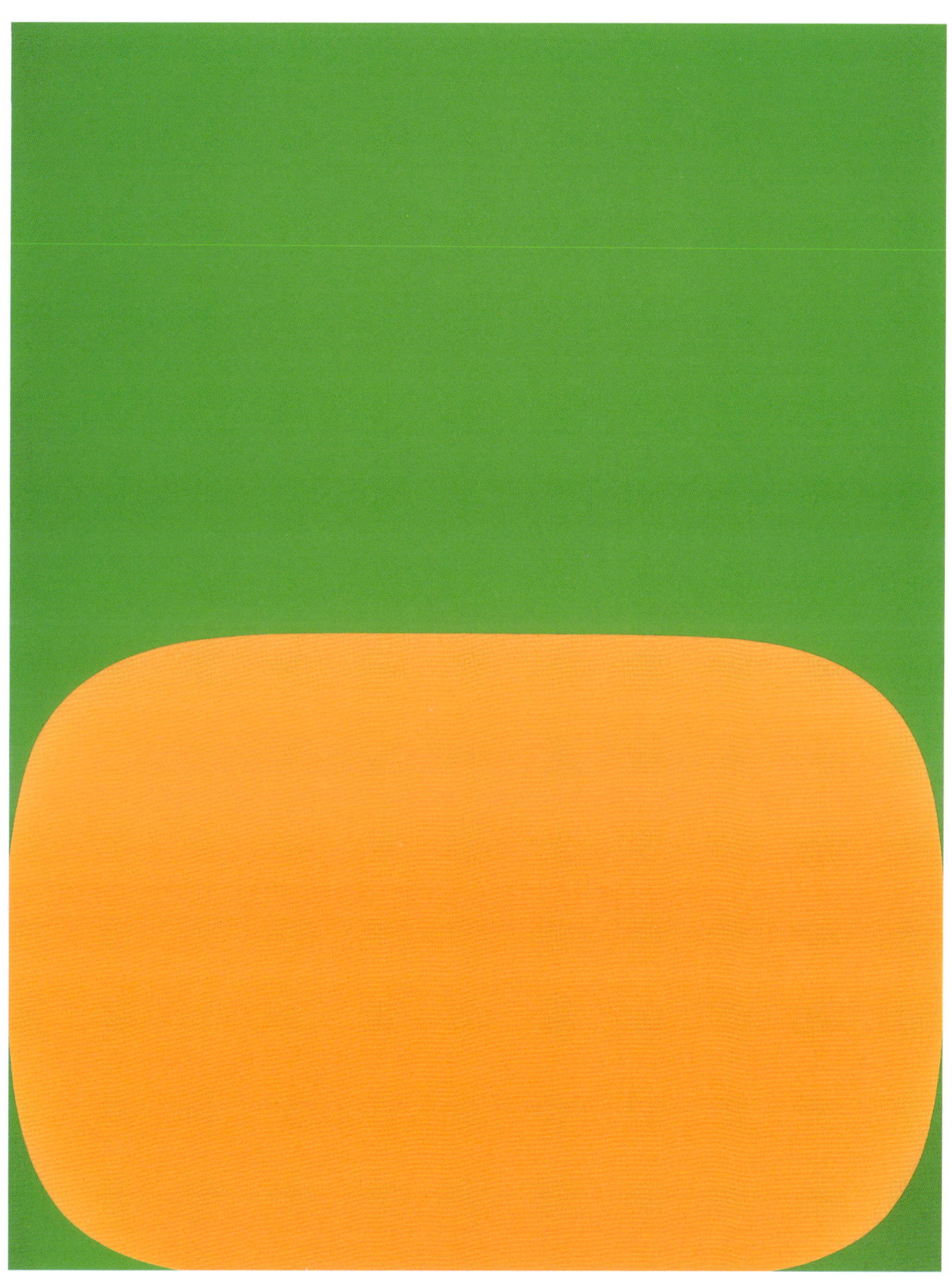

30. Ellsworth Kelly, *Orange Green*, 1966. Acrylic on canvas, 88 1/4 x 65 1/8 in. (224 x 165.4 cm). Collection of Robert and Jane Meyerhoff

ROY LICHTENSTEIN

AMERICAN, 1923–1997

Roy Lichtenstein is best known as a founder and leader of the American Pop Art movement, which took ordinary, mass-produced images from comic books, advertisements, and exhibition catalogues and turned them into cultural icons. Lichtenstein's approach to art making was remarkably consistent throughout his long career: he explored themes in a variety of media, worked in series, and moved from drawn studies through preparatory collages to finished works. A keen technical experimenter, he worked with his hands to produce seemingly anonymous surfaces. He regularly confused the distinction between abstraction and representation, creating what one commentator called "the most abstract of representational art, as well as the most representational abstractions."[1]

The *Entablatures* make up a series of thirty paintings that, as with several of his series, can be subdivided into black-and-white works (1971–1972) and works in color (1974–1976). While the artist's interest in Classical architecture can be traced back to his paintings of Greek temples from 1964, the immediate source for the *Entablatures* was a series of photographs of architectural details that he took in and around New York City's Wall Street. He shot at midday so that the elements would be crisp and sharply shadowed. Simplifying and recomposing the source photographs to create the paintings, Lichtenstein seems to ask just how few elements are needed to successfully signify cornice, frieze, and architrave, the three components (from top to bottom) of a Classical entablature.[2] In so doing, he arrives at a kind of "statistical average" of Neoclassical architecture, a bland icon filtered through the multiple lenses of early twentieth-century American architects imitating nineteenth-century French Beaux-Arts architects imitating antique models.[3] The paintings have no obvious sources in particular buildings; their subject is Neoclassicism itself. As the artist explained punningly, "This series can also be seen to represent, in a humorous way, the *establishment*. By establishment I mean that the reference in these Entablature paintings was to the Greco-Roman tradition, which permeates our art and culture."[4]

For all their references, these paintings can equally be seen as abstractions. In the Meyerhoff *Entablature*, Lichtenstein promotes this reading by filling the entire canvas with a detail, suggesting a congruence of image and field, and by emphasizing matter over illusionism. The latter is especially evident in the three silvery bands of metallic paint (a mix of sand and Magna) in the middle registers of the painting and along the top: as Lichtenstein troweled the mixture across the surface, its imperfections left long scratches. But the abstraction of the *Entablatures* is also a matter of reference. Lichtenstein explained the paintings as his "response to Minimalism and the art of Donald Judd and Kenneth Noland," noting that "the Greeks did repeated motifs early on." Indeed, the colored stripes of the *Entablatures* recall Noland's horizontal paintings, while the repetition of forms evokes the seriality and repetition of Judd's sculptures. Lichtenstein concluded, "I am showing, in a humorous way, that Minimalism has a long history."[5]

By 1983, Lichtenstein's art had changed. His signature dots, still visible in the *Entablatures*, had largely yielded in the later 1970s to stripes; his use of stencils and tape to create sharp, flat forms had become still more precise; and at the same time he had started to welcome brushed, "expressive" passages—banished long ago—back into his work.[6] All this is evident in *Painting with Statue of Liberty*, the largest of a group of paintings that combine two different styles.

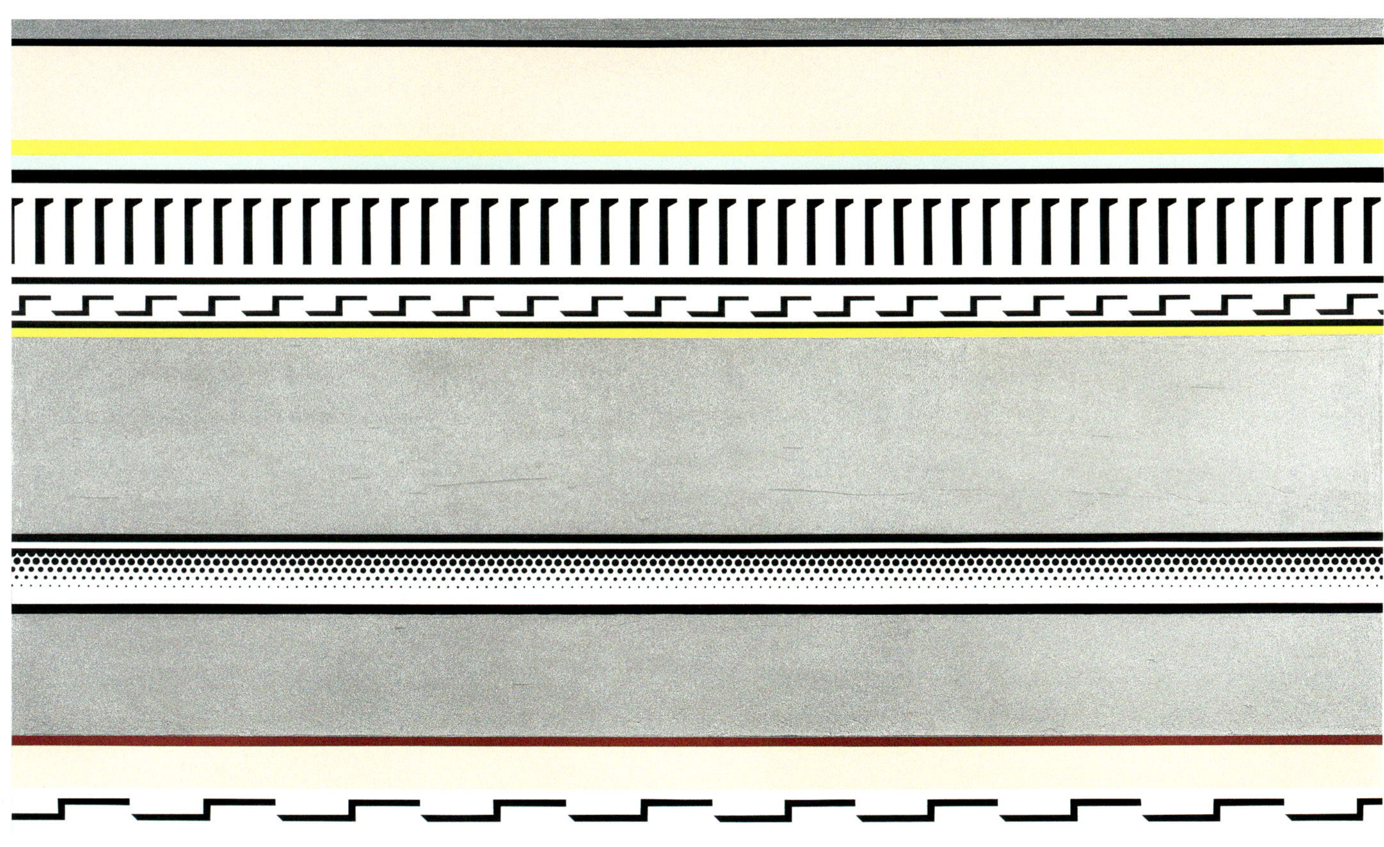

31. Roy Lichtenstein, *Entablature*, 1974. Oil, Magna, sand, Magna medium, and aluminum powder on canvas, 60 x 100 in. (152.4 x 254 cm). 2012.84.1

The right side of the painting features the Statue of Liberty, an icon of mass media, restated as a stark two-dimensional logo. (The source image is Lichtenstein's own, a screen print and poster he copublished in 1982 with People For the American Way.) The painting was carefully planned in *Two Studies for "Painting with Statue of Liberty"* (1983), also in the Meyerhoff Collection. The studies show that Lichtenstein had originally planned to contain Lady Liberty's silhouette along both the left and bottom edges of the work within a decorative frame, but in the end he eliminated the bottom frame, thus turning the remaining piece of molding into a quasi-abstract element.

The left side of the painting is a jumble of painterly brushstrokes and schematic representations of brushstrokes, scaled up to the large canvas. Lichtenstein created his *Brushstrokes* series, a group of hard-edged, cartoony paintings of brushstrokes, from 1965 to 1971, a time when the heroic ethos of Abstract Expressionism still needed puncturing. By 1983, that battle had been won, so Lichtenstein was able to include actual brushstrokes as well, except that (on closer inspection) some of them are not actual brushstrokes at all, but rather were made by dragging paint-soaked rags across the surface.

It is worth noting that Lichtenstein called the work "Painting with Statue of Liberty" instead of simply "Statue of Liberty." The title thus gives equal weight to the two parts of the work, the Abstract Expressionist brushstrokes at left and the sculpted, flattened figure at right, perhaps in order to equate the ultimate American art movement with the ultimate American logo. And yet, in the syntax of the title, the statue is secondary, a hanger-on, and indeed the central framing element is oriented to enclose not the statue but the brushstrokes. Alternatively, perhaps "painting" refers to the canvas as a whole, whose dominant attribute is the statue, just as a still life featuring a lemon might be called "Still Life with Lemon." In typical Lichtensteinian fashion, *Painting with Statue of Liberty*, like *Entablature*, forces us to think about the nature of visual, and verbal, representation.
KR

---

[1] Ruth E. Fine, "Roy Lichtenstein," in Mark Rosenthal, ed., *The Robert and Jane Meyerhoff Collection: 1945–1995*, exh. cat. (Washington, DC: National Gallery of Art, 1996), 111.

[2] This point is made by Yve-Alain Bois, "Two Birds with One Stone," in *Roy Lichtenstein: A Retrospective*, exh. cat. (Chicago: Art Institute of Chicago, 2012), 63. Select source photographs for the *Entablatures* series from the Roy Lichtenstein Foundation Archives are reproduced in this catalogue. In the Meyerhoff painting, it is noteworthy that the triglyphs (vertically channeled tablets) sit atop the dentils (a molding of projecting rectangular blocks) rather than vice versa, as is typical.

[3] Ibid.

[4] From a lecture delivered by Lichtenstein on November 11, 1995, on the occasion of being awarded the Kyoto Prize that year. See Roy Lichtenstein, "A Review of My Work since 1961—A Slide Presentation," in *Roy Lichtenstein: October Files* 7, ed. Graham Bader (Cambridge, MA: MIT Press, 2009), 66.

[5] Ibid., 66–67.

[6] The classic Benday dots appear in a central strip that bisects the two Magna registers in *Entablature* (1974). The gradually diminishing size of the dots from top to bottom creates the illusion of shadow and suggests what might be a rounded ledge. For a discussion of the evolution of the dot in Lichtenstein's practice, see Harry Cooper, "On the Dot," in *Roy Lichtenstein: A Retrospective*, 26–45.

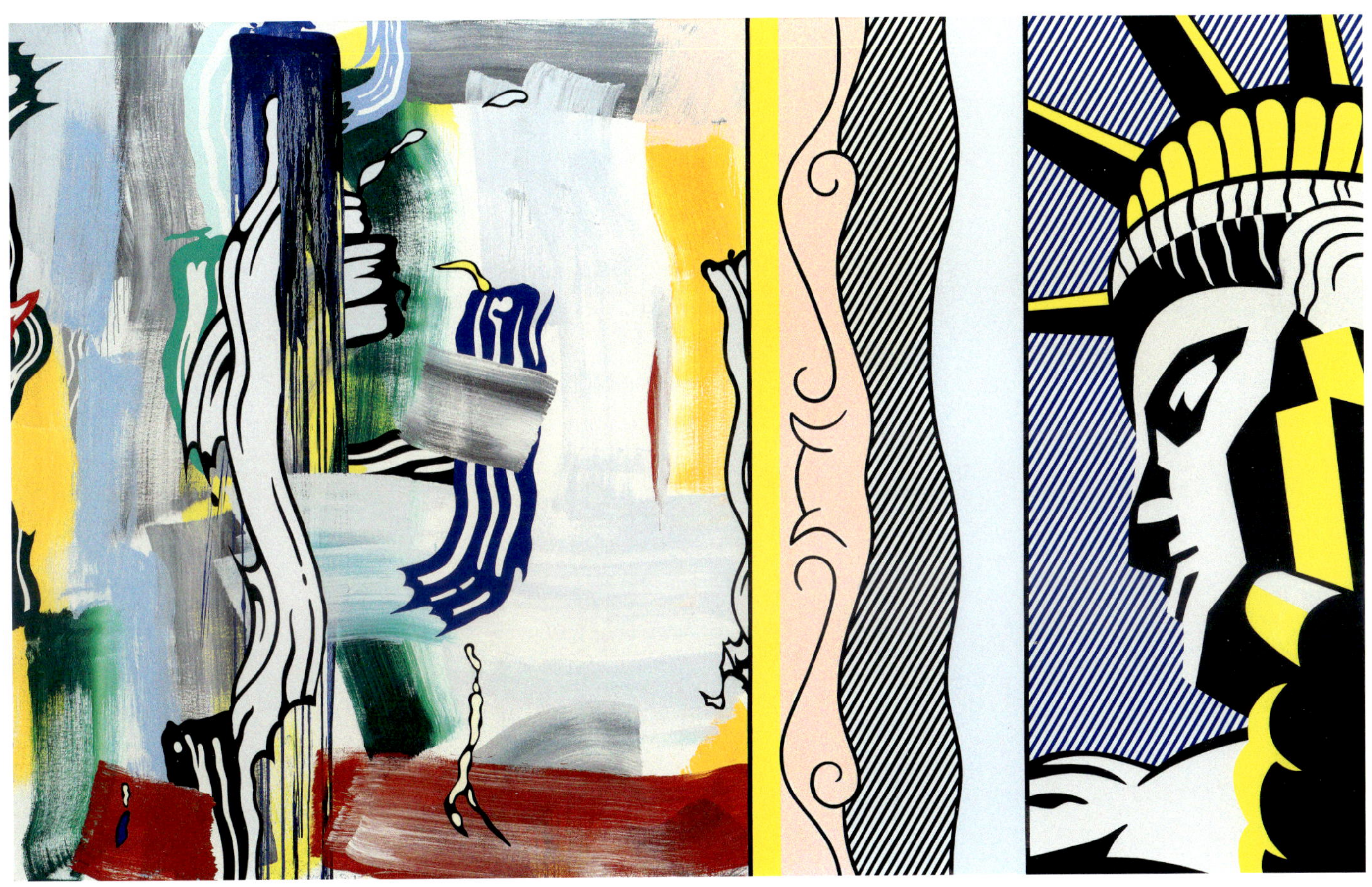

32. Roy Lichtenstein, *Painting with Statue of Liberty*, 1983. Oil and Magna on canvas, 107 x 167 in. (271.8 x 424.2 cm). 1996.81.6

BRICE MARDEN

AMERICAN, b. 1938

Brice Marden's career offers the compelling narrative of an artist who found success in the mid-1960s in a Minimalist mode, painting large monochrome canvases, and then left it all in the early 1980s for a new direction, markedly gestural and linear. Recalling the break, Marden said, "Call it a mid-life crisis. I was bored."[1] From today's perspective, it is hard to say which body of work has been more important in the history of postwar painting.

Marden moved to New York City after receiving an MFA from Yale University School of Art and Architecture in 1963. The following year, he began to make his first muted, monochromatic paintings. While working as a part-time guard at the Jewish Museum, he studied the 1964 Jasper Johns retrospective and was especially moved by the artist's use of grays and encaustic. In 1966, Marden became Robert Rauschenberg's assistant and began to show his first paintings using beeswax. He incorporated the material into a mixture of paint, turpentine, and oil that was heated in his studio and applied to the canvas with a brush. He would then repeatedly remove and reapply the paint with a spatula or palette knife until a flat, uniform, yet not entirely matte surface appeared. "The result," one critic observed, "was blank-looking paintings, with a lot to see. Their patinated surfaces transmit the warmth of old stone walls and look as if they would crack if tapped with the back of a spoon."[2]

In 1968, Marden began complicating his art by combining monochrome canvases of different colors into multi-panel paintings. He explained: "One is a universe and, you know, two just gets much, much more complex. And then when you do three, you know, it just seemed to me that making these very simple changes made for infinite possibilities."[3] In the 1970s, Marden traveled in Asia, and in 1984, he saw the exhibition *Masters of Japanese Calligraphy, 8th–9th Century* at the Asia Society in New York, which helped to further redirect his art. Precisely because he could not read Japanese or Chinese calligraphy, the artist came to appreciate its marks as abstract, gymnastic, lyrical: "Calligraphy is very personal because it is very physical. It's not a technique or an ideology; it's a form of pure expression."[4] Inspired, Marden began to fill his canvases with open networks, matrices, and webs of twisted, linear strokes executed with long brushes.

Picasso's Skull exemplifies Marden's newfound approach. The painting consists of two equal-sized canvases joined together; the ground color of the one on the right has been scraped away more, which gives it a paler hue than the one on the left. A dense mesh of lines, composed of two shades each of dull yellow, bluish gray, and brownish black, moves freely across the divide. Many of the lines have been scraped down too, giving the whole a weathered, muted appearance that may owe something to Marden's interests in scholar's rocks and ceramic glazes. What might at first seem to be a random set of lines in fact has its own stately rhythm and structure, turning away from the edges or running along them and forming vertical columns (see the light gray in particular) that derive from the columnar form of couplets in Chinese poetry. Behind these immediate sources, like a muffled undercurrent, runs the example of Jackson Pollock's poured paintings, with their allover webs of thrown lines.

Regarding the title of the work, *Picasso's Skull*, Marden remarked, "There is somewhere in there an image that reminded me very much of the late self-portrait he did. . . . And then also his skull, the war-time skull he did is my favorite Picasso piece. . . . It was there someplace but it was very early on in the painting. This was painted [for] a long time. It has a lot of colors, a lot of layers. It got very complicated but it was in there."[5]

PR

---

1 Brice Marden, quoted in Paul Gardner, "Call It a Mid-Life Crisis," *ARTnews* 93, no. 4 (April 1994): 140.

2 Paul Taylor, "Marden's Metamorphosis," *Connoisseur* 221, no. 957 (October 1991): 25.

3 Brice Marden, in conversation with Harry Cooper, "The Diamonstein-Spielvogel Lecture Series: Brice Marden on Art," National Gallery of Art, Washington, Sunday Lecture Transcripts, November 22, 2009, 10.

4 Brice Marden, interview by Lilly Wei, "Talking Abstract," *Art in America* 75, no. 7 (July 1987): 83.

5 Marden, "The Diamonstein-Spielvogel Lecture Series," 28.

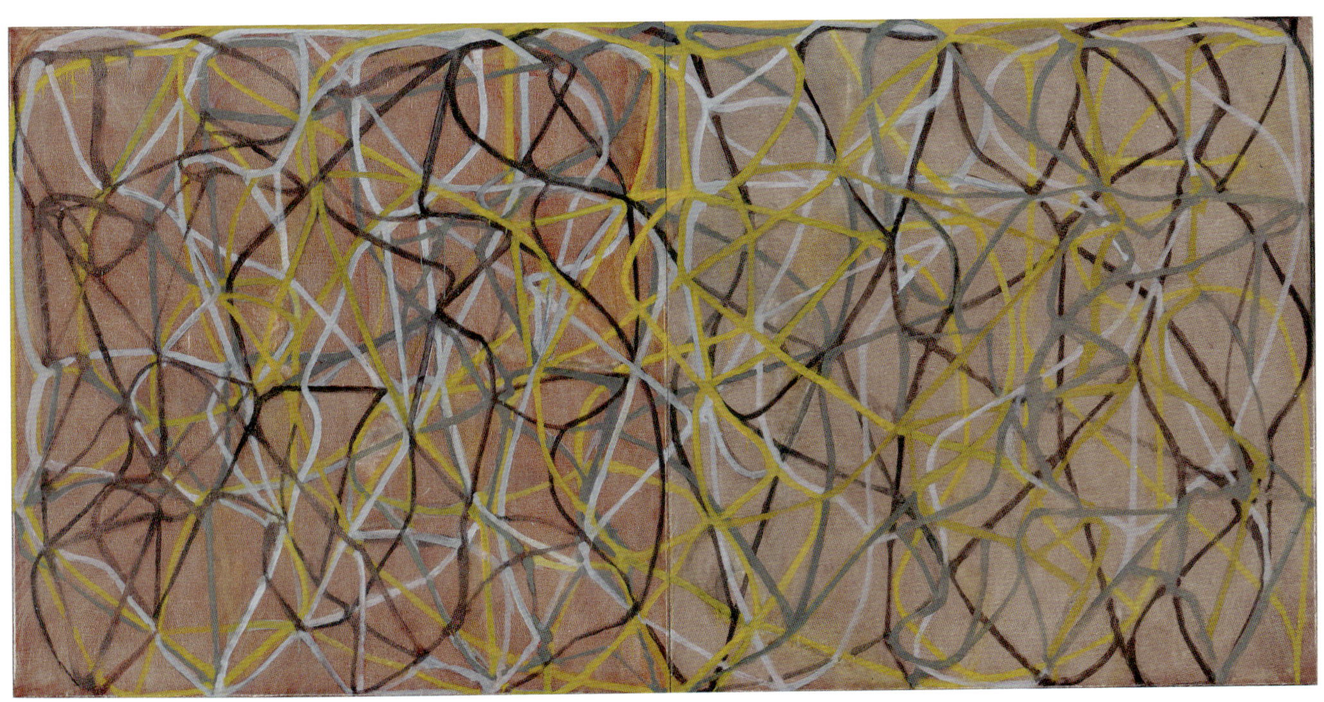

33. Brice Marden, *Picasso's Skull*, 1989–1990. Oil on linen (two joined panels), overall: 62 x 120 in. (157.5 x 304.8 cm). Collection of Robert and Jane Meyerhoff

AGNES MARTIN

AMERICAN, b. CANADA, 1912–2004

Throughout her long career, Agnes Martin remained steadfast in the conviction that abstract painting could provide a profound, uniquely meditative experience. During the 1950s and early 1960s, Martin lived in New York, where she absorbed the currents of Pop art and Minimalism, filling her canvases and drawings with representational images and biomorphic abstractions before arriving at simple geometric shapes as well as dots, dashes, and bands. During a seven-year hiatus from painting, she visited New Mexico, where she had previously lived while a student and teacher, and finally settled there in 1967. Leaving New York behind, Martin adopted a spartan lifestyle that matched the austerity of her paintings. Although she is often associated with Minimalism, Martin belonged to the generation of Abstract Expressionists (she was the same age as Jackson Pollock) and felt she had more in common with their outlook.

The painting *Untitled #2* derives from the later phase of Martin's mature work. The square 72-by-72-inch format is typical. Horizontal lines drawn with blue pencil span the stretched and primed canvas, just reaching the edge. The spaces between many of the lines are filled with either pale blue or a shade of peach; between other lines, only the white-gessoed canvas is seen. While there is no regular pattern to the colored bands, they appear as five distinct registers, each consisting of a varying pattern of twelve bands: four peach, four blue, and four white. Four bands of white surround each cluster. This varied yet repetitive structure demands our engagement and solicits our desire for order while refusing to offer any particular points of focus.

Although her art went through several changes, including a late return to larger shapes, Martin essentially made square paintings based on grids or rows of lines from 1962 until her death in 2004. This vocabulary was the vehicle for her philosophy, which she recorded in careful writing on lined notebook paper. At the center of her ideas stood the viewer. As she stated in 1973, "The life of the work depends upon the observer according to his own awareness of perfection and inspiration."[1] But perfection was a goal, not a reality: "I hope I have made it clear that the work is *about* perception as we are aware of it in our own minds but that the paintings are very far from being perfect—completely removed in fact—even as we ourselves are."[2]

PR

---

[1] Agnes Martin, "Reflections," *Artforum* 11, no. 8 (April 1973): 38.

[2] Agnes Martin, *Agnes Martin: Writings / Schriften*, ed. Dieter Schwartz (Winterthur: Kunstmuseum Winterthur in association with Edition Cantz, 1991), 15.

34. Agnes Martin, *Untitled #2*, 1981. Acrylic and blue pencil on canvas, 72 x 72 in. (182.9 x 182.9 cm). 1992.28.6

ROBERT RAUSCHENBERG

AMERICAN, 1925–2008

Robert Rauschenberg was a protean figure, constantly collaborating and crossing media boundaries while finding new ways to incorporate the world into his work and vice versa. Beginning in the 1950s, Rauschenberg and fellow Neo-Dadaist Jasper Johns drew inspiration from advertising, commodities, everyday objects, and found materials, developing images that prefigured Pop Art by a decade and opened the way for countless other innovations. As art historian Robert Rosenblum commented, "Every artist after 1960 who challenged the restrictions of painting and sculpture and believed that all of life was open to art is indebted to Rauschenberg—forever."[1]

Rauschenberg grew up in modest circumstances in Port Arthur, Texas, and soon embarked on a peripatetic life. He served in the Navy, and then attended the Kansas City Art Institute for one year under the G.I. Bill. After a trip to Paris, he entered Black Mountain College in North Carolina in 1948, where he studied with Josef Albers. In 1949, he moved to New York, where he took classes periodically at the Art Students League. His all-black and all-white paintings date from this period. While traveling through Europe and North Africa in the early 1950s, Rauschenberg collected bones, sticks, and other oddities, fashioning them into *scatole contemplative* (thought boxes). Upon his return to New York, he embraced color, covering canvases of collaged items (newspaper, printed paper, fabric) with red paint. In 1954, Rauschenberg introduced actual objects into the Red paintings, and the Combines were born. Taxidermied animals, street signs, doors, mirrors, pillows, and tires poured into these "paintings," which at times left the wall, becoming freestanding constructions.

In the late 1950s, Rauschenberg became equally interested in the appropriation of two-dimensional images; in 1958, he developed a solvent technique that allowed him to transfer printed material directly onto his drawings. In 1962, inspired by Andy Warhol's use of the process, he began silkscreening images onto canvas. After choosing images from magazines and newspapers, he would send them to a company that created silkscreens via a photographic process. By 1963, Rauschenberg had moved from black and white to color silkscreening. He appreciated the element of surprise in the process:

> When I get the screens back from the manufacturer the images on them look different from the way they did in the original photographs, because of the change in scale, so that's one surprise right there. Then, they look different again when I transfer them to canvas, so there's another surprise. And they keep on suggesting different things when they're juxtaposed with other images on the canvas, so there's the same kind of interaction that goes on in the combines and the same possibilities of collaboration and discovery.[2]

Archive is an important early example of this method. The canvas is strewn with diverse images, often rotated or inverted, including a wrought iron fence, Boy Scouts marching with American flags, a military helicopter, airplane control panels, bathers on a beach, and a highway overpass. Gestural strokes of paint animate the canvas, in some places thick and opaque, in others transparent. And yet there is a quite traditional order in this disorder: an underlying grid, that recurring figure in modernist abstraction, both organizes the images and is depicted in some of them. The central red blob creates a strong point of focus, surrounded by blues and greens, which are, in turn, framed at top and bottom by warmer tones of orange and brown. Many of the images relate to movement and transportation, and their mix of patriotism and militarism suggests the growing unrest that would soon mark the entire decade.

PR

---

1 Robert Rosenblum, quoted in Robert Hughes, "The Most Living Artist," *Time*, November 29, 1976, 54.

2 Robert Rauschenberg, quoted in Calvin Tomkins, *The Bride and the Bachelors: The Heretical Courtship in Modern Art* (New York: Viking Press, 1965), 233.

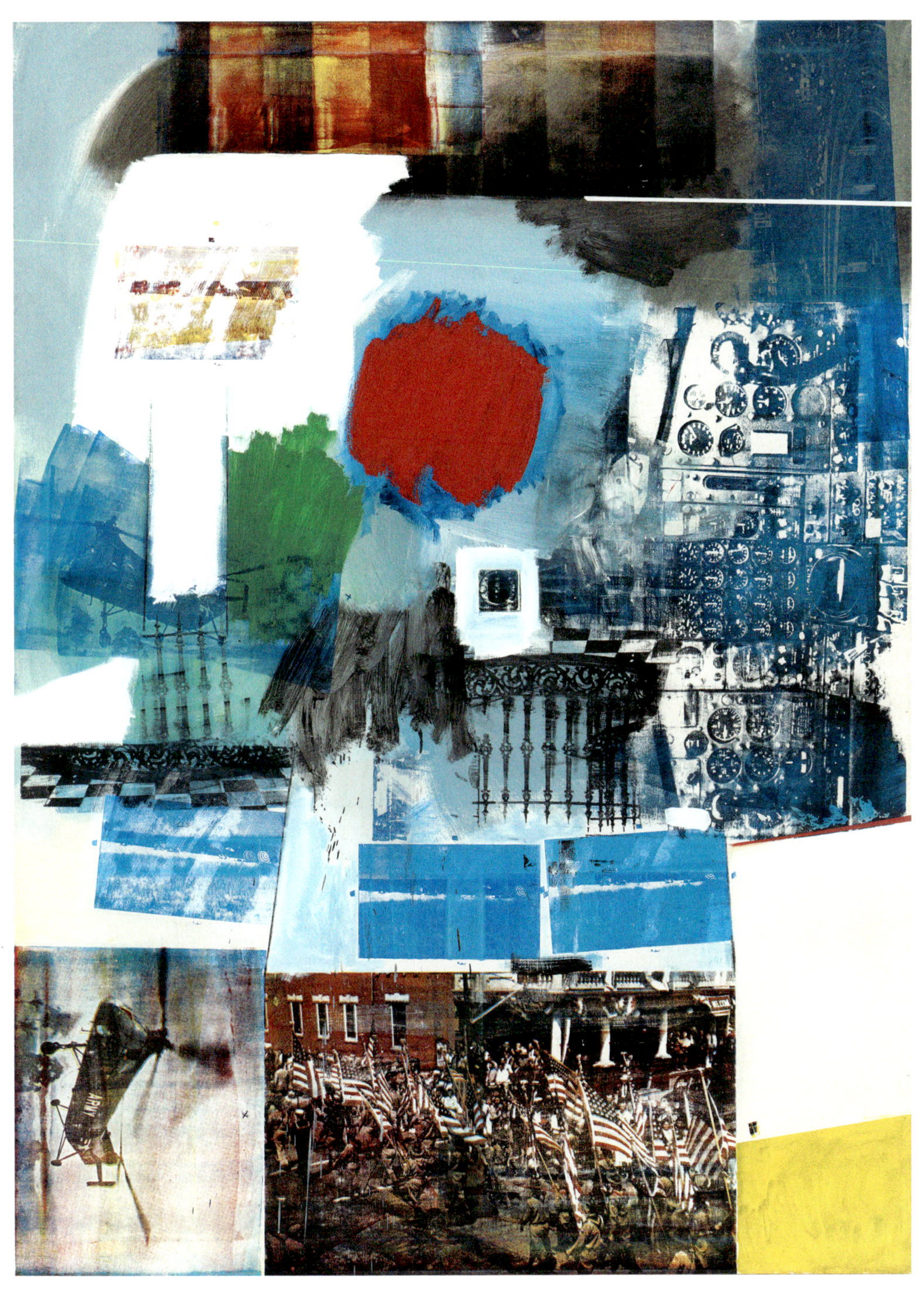

35. Robert Rauschenberg, *Archive*, 1963. Oil and silkscreen ink on canvas, 84 x 60 in. (213.4 x 152.4 cm). Collection of the Robert and Jane Meyerhoff Art Foundation, Inc.

AD REINHARDT

AMERICAN, 1913–1967

Known as the "black monk" for his near-monochrome paintings of dark grids that refuse all meanings and associations, Ad Reinhardt was a singular figure, one impossible to classify. His work was an important stimulus to the Minimalist artists of the 1960s, but his commitment to painting rather than object making meant that he had little in common with them. His peers were the Abstract Expressionists, yet he had no patience for their spiritual and political claims. He was simply an abstract painter, and stubbornly identified himself as such.[1]

Born in Buffalo, New York, and raised in Brooklyn and Queens, Reinhardt studied art history with Meyer Schapiro at Columbia University from 1931 to 1935. After graduation, he trained as a painter at the National Academy of Design and the American Artists School, and also took graduate classes in Asian art history at the Institute of Fine Arts. From 1936 to 1941, he worked for the Federal Art Project of the New Deal, as did many artists of his era. Staunchly opposed to figurative imagery of any kind, he was a member of the American Abstract Artists organization.

During the early 1940s, influenced by Stuart Davis and Carl Holty, Reinhardt made brightly colored collages and paintings in a geometric abstract manner.[2] By mid-decade, he had begun to exhibit his work in New York and to publish biting cartoons about the art world; the latter made him few friends. His work of the later 1940s explored a variety of devices: allover compositions, fragmented calligraphy, hazy fields, and tesserae of color arranged in loose grids. By 1950, Reinhardt's motifs had grown large, broad, and flat, establishing stable relationships to the edges of the canvas, with simple colors high in saturation and contrast.

Untitled (Red and Gray) and *Untitled (Yellow and White)*, a pair of paintings from 1950, exploit close values and interlocking shapes to create visually disturbing patterns that confuse figure and ground. In *Red and Gray*, Reinhardt employed a broad brush to apply a neutral gray on top of a hot red ground; in *Yellow and White*, he painted a brilliant yellow on top of the primed canvas. The optical effects are electric, adding to the difficulty of determining which color is on top of the other, whether actually or illusionistically.

Despite the purity of the binary relationships in these canvases, their soft edges betray what one commentator called a "residual regard for abstract expressionist effects, especially in the work of Mark Rothko and, more distantly, Clyfford Still."[3]

In retrospect, Reinhardt's circa-1950 work reveals itself as a step in the gradual reduction of his art, which soon led to his exile of figure-ground relations and brushwork of any kind, his embrace of symmetry, and his obsession with close contrast.[4] He first made these rigorous paintings in shades of blue or red, and they were often vertical in format. They culminated in the Black paintings, which would occupy him until his death in 1967. With these "ultimate" paintings (Reinhardt's term), difficult to see and impossible to reproduce, he fused his art and his aesthetics, concentrating the viewer's attention on gradations at the threshold of visibility. Reinhardt explained his distillation of pictorial means in 1962: "The one thing to say about art is that it is one thing. Art is art-as-art and everything else is everything else. Art-as-art is nothing but art. Art is not what is not art."[5]

KR

---

[1] In 1965, Richard Wollheim acknowledged the Black paintings of Reinhardt as a seminal influence on the evolution of Minimal Art. See Richard Wollheim, "Minimal Art," *Arts Magazine* (January 1965): 26–32. See also Barbara Rose, "ABC Art," *Art in America* 35, no. 5 (October–November 1965): 57–69, repr. in *Minimal Art: A Critical Anthology*, ed. Gregory Battcock (New York: E. P. Dutton, 1968), 277–297. For a contemporary discussion of Minimal readings of Reinhardt, see Michael Corris, "Reinhardt and the Art of the Sixties," in *Ad Reinhardt* (London: Reaktion, 2008), 129–148.

[2] Davis and Reinhardt had neighboring studios for a time. See "Chronology," in Lucy R. Lippard and Sam Hunter, *Ad Reinhardt: Paintings*, exh. cat. (New York: Jewish Museum, 1967), 34.

[3] Marla Prather, "Ad Reinhardt," in Mark Rosenthal, ed., *The Robert and Jane Meyerhoff Collection: 1945–1995*, exh. cat. (Washington, DC: National Gallery of Art, 1996), 185. See also Lucy R. Lippard, *Ad Reinhardt* (New York: Harry N. Abrams, 1981), 83.

[4] Reinhardt's exposure to the work of Piet Mondrian and his contact with Josef Albers, with whom he taught at Yale from 1952 to 1953, may have been catalysts for his turn to stricter geometry. See Lippard, *Ad Reinhardt*, 18–22.

[5] Ad Reinhardt, "Art-as-Art," *Art International* 6, no. 10 (December 1962), repr. in *Art-as-Art: The Selected Writings of Ad Reinhardt*, ed. Barbara Rose (New York: Viking Press, 1975), 53.

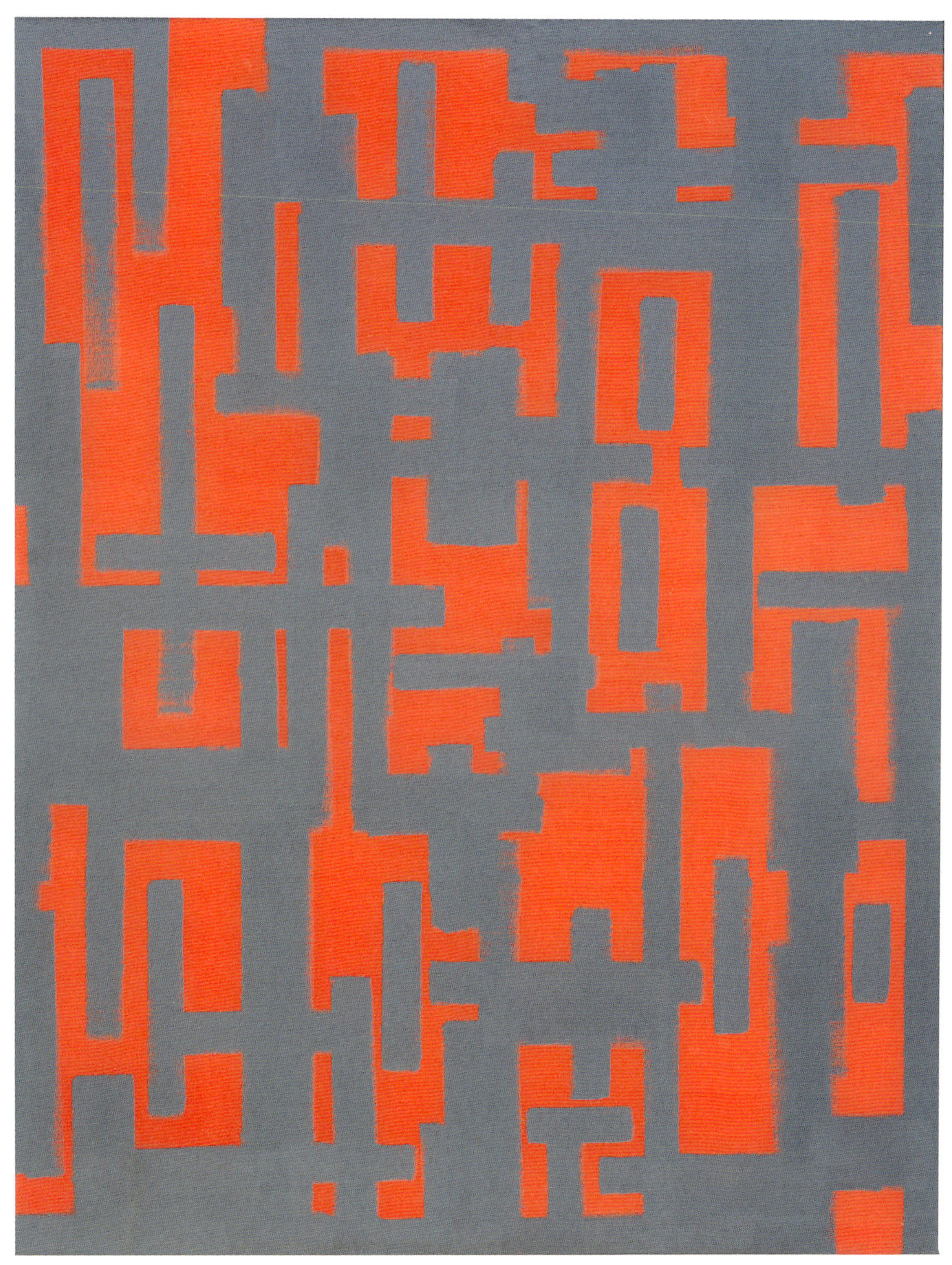

36. Ad Reinhardt, *Untitled (Red and Gray)*, 1950. Oil on canvas, 80 x 60 in. (203.2 x 152.4 cm). 1992.28.3

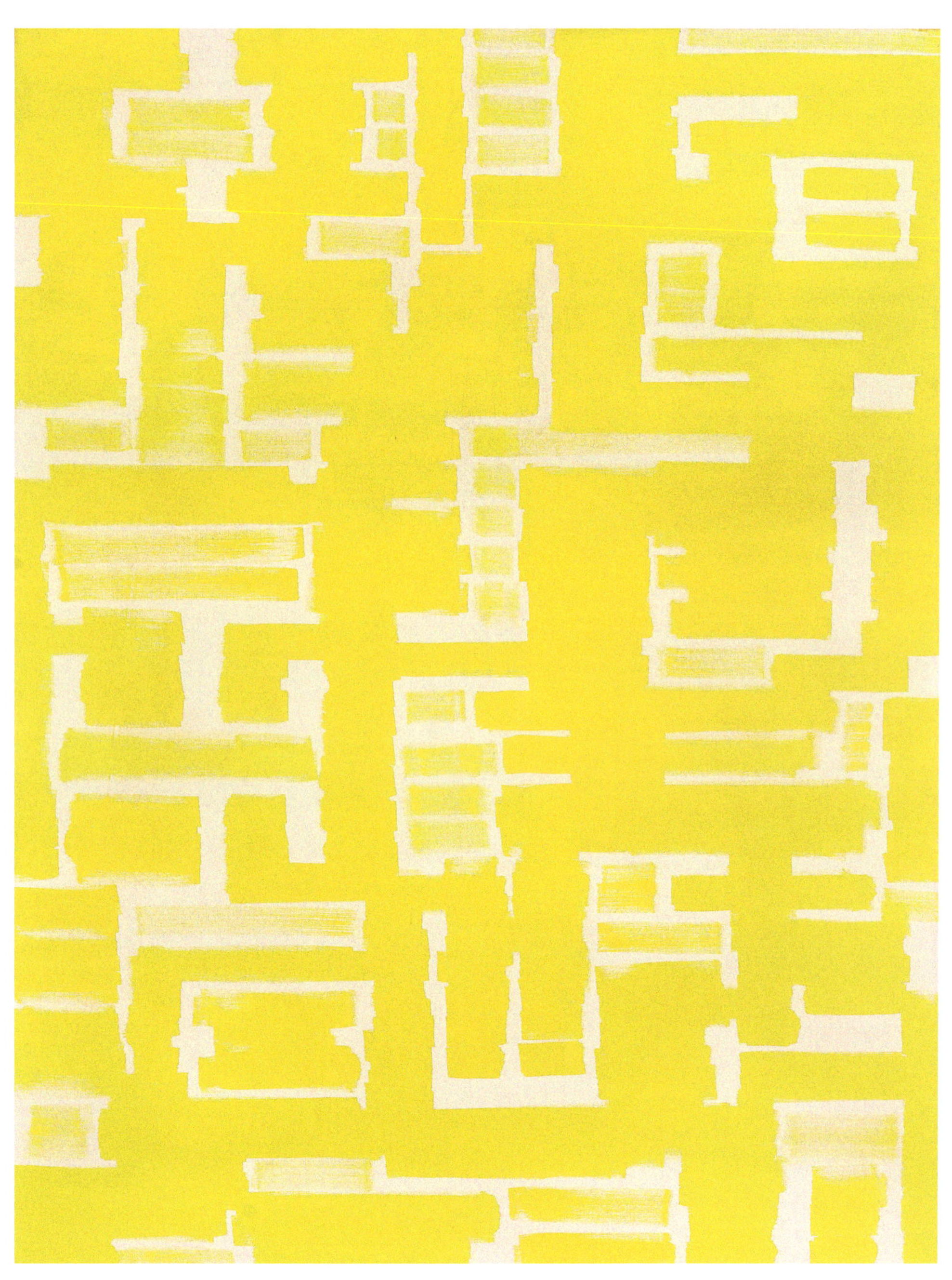

37. Ad Reinhardt, *Untitled (Yellow and White)*, 1950. Oil on canvas, 80 x 60 in. (203.2 x 152.4 cm). 1992.28.2

JAMES ROSENQUIST

AMERICAN, b. 1933

James Rosenquist gained recognition in the early 1960s for paintings that juxtaposed disparate commercial images and altered their scale and context. A former billboard painter who began to use the visual vocabulary of advertising in his art, Rosenquist made cutouts from magazines and ads, assembled them in enigmatic juxtapositions, enlarged them using a grid, and executed them as large-scale paintings. As a leading Pop artist alongside Andy Warhol and Roy Lichtenstein, he aimed to respond to contemporary life without the personal gestures of his Abstract Expressionist predecessors.

Spectator - Speed of Light is the work of the mature Rosenquist, who had come to a broader view of art history and his place in it:

> In deciding to do the Speed of Light [series of] paintings [in 1999], I thought, where do I go from here? Well, I went back to color and form in a different way than in my previous work. Pop art was a reaction to the drips, splashes, and smears of the abstract expressionists. When I look at those works now, the splashes, drips, and smears seem amazingly avant-garde. They don't look redundant anymore; they look historical, shocking, and very delicate, especially in the work of Kline, Pollock, and de Kooning. But when your teachers are telling you to do this and that, you react against it, and that's what Pop art was. Then, as time goes by, your mind may be introduced again to something you glossed over in the past.[1]

Rosenquist has always painted by hand, and close viewing of his seemingly impersonal surfaces reveals a surprising degree of brushwork. This is especially true of *Spectator - Speed of Light*. Seen from a distance, the painting depicts a reflective, sharp-edged metallic ribbon that twists and turns in space as it reflects what may be colorful patterns of wallpaper behind it. Viewed at close range, everything dissolves into a freely brushed abstraction of lines and splotches. Rosenquist earlier had explored abstraction in his Pop works of the 1960s: their imagery was cropped, scaled up or down, and edited so as to make it almost illegible. This may have reflected his experience as a young billboard painter, when he could not step back to see the entire image while working on a given passage.

The title *Spectator - Speed of Light* references Albert Einstein's special theory of relativity (1905), which holds that to a slower-moving spectator, someone traveling near the speed of light would appear to exist in a world of dilated time and compressed dimension. While an artistic representation of that idea is impossible, Rosenquist's painting can be read as a visual analogue to the theory: the shiny band represents the speeding world, with its warping and dislocation, as seen from the perspective of a relatively stationary observer, himself represented by the more legible patterns on the white ground.

Rosenquist suggested a parallel between Einstein's theory and his own experience as a painter: "What you see is *not* what you get. The painting is really the archaeology of all my intellect, practice and production. You can't see all the machinations I've gone through to arrive at this point of reference."[2] He warns us that there is a great divide between our experience as observers of a single work and the speed and density of his career. This divide may indeed be part of Rosenquist's subject.[3]

KR

---

[1] James Rosenquist, in conversation with Sarah Bancroft, August and September 2006, quoted in Bancroft, "From Abstraction and Back Again, Traveling at the Speed of Light," in Bancroft et al., *James Rosenquist*, exh. cat. (London: Haunch of Venison Gallery, 2006), 112.

[2] Ibid.

[3] See also Sarah Bancroft, "Space and Scientific Phenomena," in Walter Hopps et al., *James Rosenquist: A Retrospective*, exh. cat. (New York: Solomon R. Guggenheim Museum, 2003), 230.

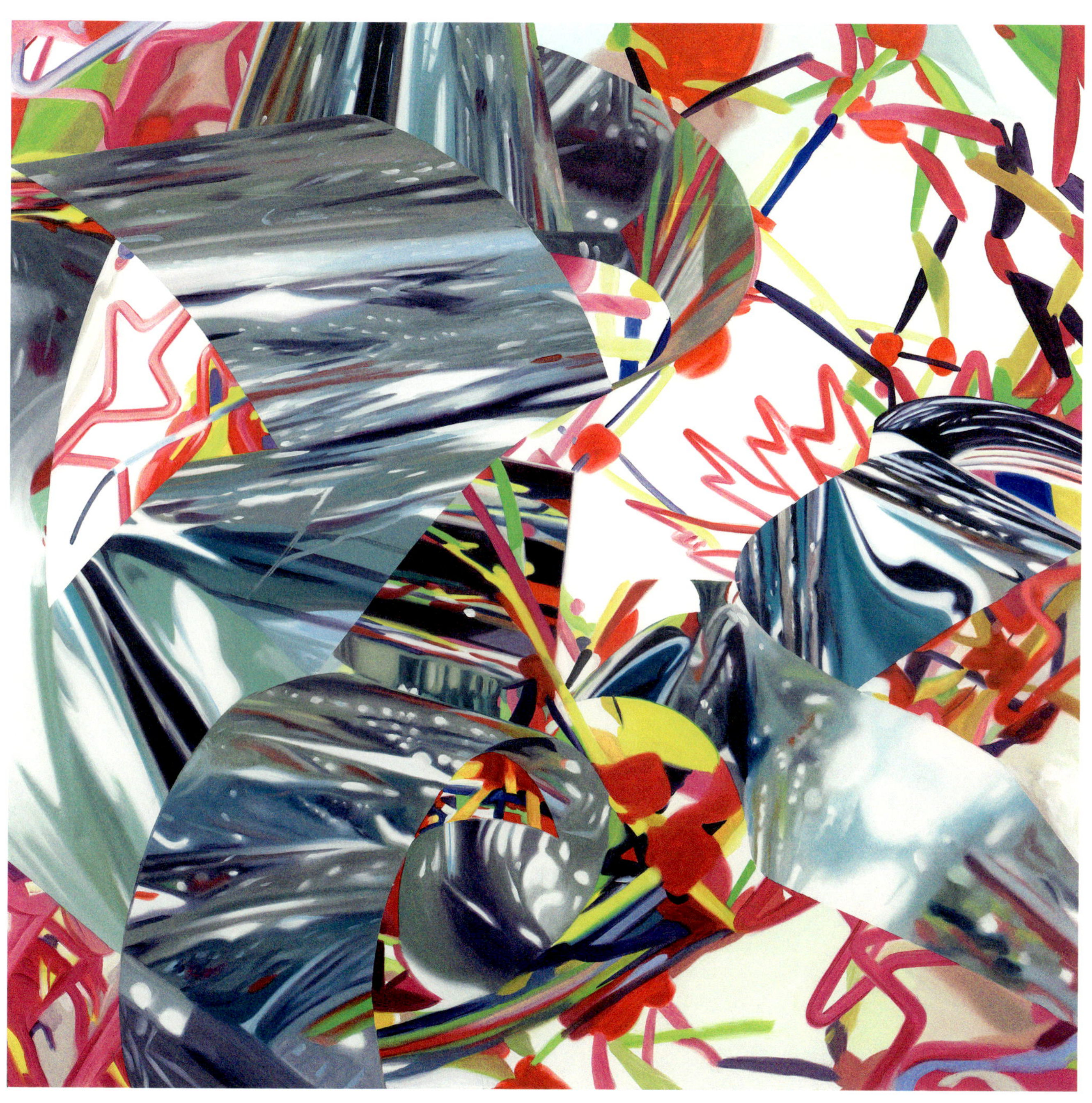

38. James Rosenquist, *Spectator - Speed of Light*, 2001. Oil on linen, 72 x 72 in. (182.9 x 182.9 cm). 2010.14.2

MARK ROTHKO

AMERICAN, b. RUSSIA, 1903–1970

Born Marcus Rothkowitz in Russia (now Latvia), Mark Rothko emigrated with his family to the United States in 1913 at the age of ten.[1] After attending Yale University for two years, he moved to New York, where he soon discovered an interest in painting and drawing and took classes at the Art Students League. His works of the 1920s and 1930s depict figures, landscapes, and still lifes in a blocky, expressive style that owed much to the example of his mentor, American painter Milton Avery. During the 1930s, Rothko's work began to reflect contemporary urban life and perhaps his own left-leaning politics. Many of the figures in his subway stations and city scenes appear isolated and attenuated, suggesting the plight of humanity in the modern world. Even in this early work, the space within his canvases is often divided by horizontal bands, "an underlying, if often subliminal, unifying factor throughout Rothko's oeuvre."[2]

During the early 1940s, Rothko's scenes were infused with references to Classical myth and architecture, reflecting his interest in Greek drama and his reading of Friedrich Nietzsche's *The Birth of Tragedy* (1872). By the mid-1940s, his compositions had become more abstract under the influence of Surrealism, and he found inspiration in the suggestive surfaces of his flowing and scraped watercolors. In the series of 1947–1948 known as the Multiforms, abstract, amoeba-like shapes slowly organize into the tiered rectangles that would become his trademark from 1949 onward.

To achieve the radiance that characterizes his art, Rothko made his own paints, mixing powdered pigments with glue, eggs, and oil. He used big, floppy brushes to achieve the feathered edges and translucent surfaces of his fields. The result is at once a declaration and a dissolution of surface.

The viewer's experience was essential to Rothko and his creative vision: "I realize that historically the function of painting large pictures is painting something very grandiose and pompous. The reason I paint them, however . . . is precisely because I want to be very intimate and human."[3] He wanted to create a physical relationship with the viewer in the hope of inspiring a spiritual experience: "I'm interested only in expressing basic human emotions—tragedy, ecstasy, doom and so on—and the fact that lots of people break down and cry when confronted with my pictures shows that I *communicate* those basic human emotions. . . . The people who weep before my pictures are having the same religious experience I had when I painted them."[4]

As the 1950s advanced, Rothko began to modify his palette, employing darker shades of blue, black, purple, and red. He also became more concerned with the installation of his work, favoring dim lighting and close viewing distances. Hoping that his works would exist together within an environment, he accepted commissions to fill large interiors at the Four Seasons Restaurant in New York, Harvard University, and a chapel in Houston.

After suffering a heart attack and struggling with depression in 1968, Rothko began working with acrylics, and he sometimes worked on paper, utilizing a smaller scale than his earlier paintings. *Untitled* (1969) is an example of the Black on Gray paintings, the last series of full-size works on canvas made before his death. Two rectangular blocks of color, one black and the other sepia, are divided by a soft line of brushstrokes. The lower rectangle is cool and dark in some areas, rusty and almost brown in others. The rectangles no longer float within a colored border, as in Rothko's classic work, but fill the surface except for a slim, sharp margin, resulting from taping along the edges of the canvas.

PR

---

[1] He changed his name in 1940 for the show *New Work by Marcel Gromaire, Mark Rothko, Joseph Solman* at Neumann-Willard Gallery in New York. The change did not become legal until 1959.

[2] Diane Waldman, "Mark Rothko: The Farther Shore of Art," in *Mark Rothko, 1903–1970: A Retrospective*, exh. cat. (New York: Solomon R. Guggenheim Museum, 1978), 60.

[3] Mark Rothko, statement, "A Symposium on How to Combine Architecture, Painting, and Sculpture," The Museum of Modern Art, New York, March 19, 1951, repr. in "Selected Writings and Statements by Rothko," in *The Rothko Book*, ed. Bonnie Clearwater (London: Tate Publishing, 2006), 185.

[4] Mark Rothko, "Note from a Conversation with Selden Rodman, 1956," in *Writings on Art/Mark Rothko*, ed. Miguel López-Remiro (New Haven, CT: Yale University Press, 2006), 119–120.

39. Mark Rothko, *Untitled*, 1969. Acrylic on canvas, 102 x 89 1/4 in. (259.1 x 226.7 cm). Collection of Robert and Jane Meyerhoff

DAVID SALLE

AMERICAN, b. 1952

Deploying a variety of subjects within a single canvas, including popular culture, art history, erotica, and everyday objects, and adopting styles from Photorealism to abstraction, David Salle forces viewers to confront and question the nature of representation. His work has been called "a symptomatic illustration of the bewildering visual repertoire of modern man and civilization."[1] His approach recalls the device of montage in films, only in Salle's work the sequence is compressed into a single moment, a fractured tableau.

Born in Norman, Oklahoma, Salle studied with John Baldessari, among others, at the California Institute of the Arts in the early 1970s. He moved to New York City in time to become part of the circle around Artists Space, where the seminal 1977 exhibition *Pictures* (which included Robert Longo and Sherrie Levine, but not Salle) marked a resurgence of various kinds of figurative art. Salle's paintings belong more to the Conceptual than to the Neo-Expressionist vein of this return: his influences include Sigmar Polke and Gerhard Richter, who reconfigured the commodity-based Pop image, as well as the late figurative paintings of Dada pioneer Francis Picabia, which border on kitsch.

Coming and Going consists of separate scenes on four panels closely joined to form a single large rectangle. The upper horizontal panel spotlights several objects painted with a cursory realism: a simple candlestick; a sculpted bust resembling Alberto Giacometti's *Grande tête de Diego* (1954); two green ceramic vases, which Salle has identified as "something Futurist Italian"; and a strange vessel, possibly in the shape of a duck, which he recalls as "something from the Bauhaus."[2] The lower part of the composition is composed of three vertical canvases of different sizes. At left, occupying two of the panels, is a black-and-white reproduction of a woman playing accordion while a group of men at a bar look on; the image is appropriated from Robert Doisneau's 1953 photograph *Les bouchers mélomanes* (translated as "The Music-Loving Butchers"), taken in Les Halles in Paris. Superimposed on this image lies a screen of patterned flowers outlined in blue, suggesting wallpaper, while a brown eye, located centrally but easy to miss, erupts between the men and the accordionist. In the right panel, a female nude reclining at a provocative angle is painted in grisaille.

Many of the images in *Coming and Going* originate from an archive that Salle incorporates throughout his oeuvre. Floating eyes occur in several paintings of the same era, including *The Kelly Bag* (1987) and *Landscape with Two Nudes and Three Eyes* (1986). The nude figure is present in many works, sometimes juxtaposed with depictions of bronze sculptures, as in *Fooling with Your Hair* (1985). But Salle alters these images as context demands. For instance, his decision to render the "Bauhaus" vessel in shades of red and white suggests a side of beef that the butchers below might have carved. (In *Salt Banners* [1985], a similar vessel is rendered in different colors.)[3] While such connections can be traced and references assigned, Salle's complex imagery demands multiple readings. "The task of assigning meaning is transferred to the viewer, but as Salle knows and emphasizes, no single interpretation can be devised."[4]

PR

---

[1] Klaus Honnef, *Contemporary Art* (Cologne: Taschen,1988), 181.

[2] David Salle, letter to Jeffrey Weiss, May 25, 1995, curatorial files, Department of Modern Art, National Gallery of Art, Washington.

[3] Jeffrey Weiss suggested the similar shape of the object in *Salt Banners*. Jeffrey Weiss, "David Salle," in Mark Rosenthal, ed., *The Robert and Jane Meyerhoff Collection: 1945–1995*, exh. cat. (Washington, DC: National Gallery of Art, 1996), 194.

[4] Kristin Olive, "David Salle's Deconstructive Strategy," *Arts Magazine* 60, no. 3 (November 1985): 83.

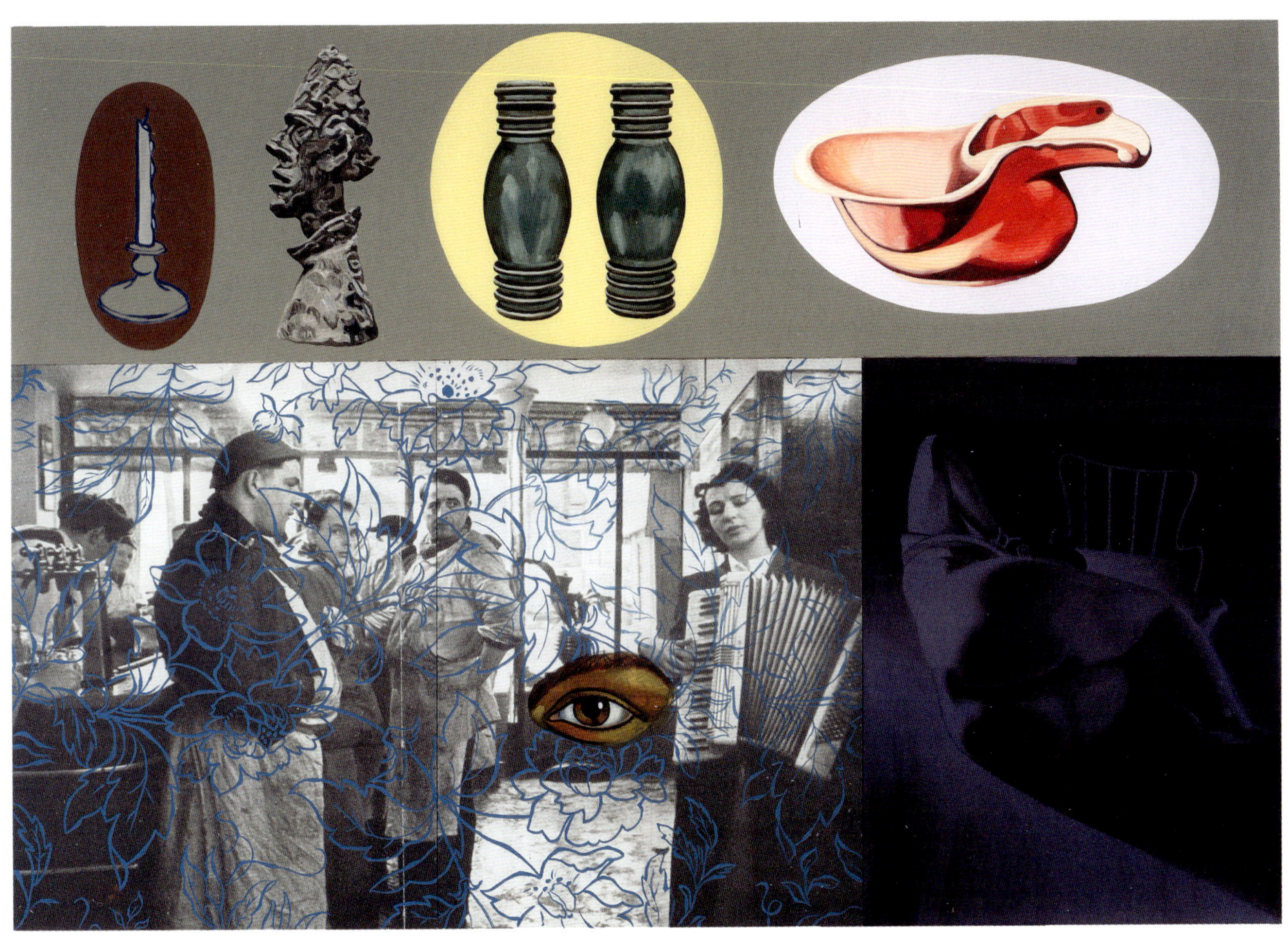

40. David Salle, *Coming and Going*, 1987. Acrylic and oil on photosensitized canvas (four joined panels), overall: 96 x 133 5/8 in. (243.8 x 339.4 cm). 1994.82.5

FRANK STELLA

AMERICAN, b. 1936

Over a long career still very much in progress, Frank Stella has repeatedly reinvented his art and, with it, the landscape of abstract painting and sculpture. Initially famous for his Black paintings, a group of works that did much to inspire Minimalist sculpture, Stella steadily broadened his palette and compositional range through many series, eventually reaching almost baroque heights of scale and complexity that seemed to contradict his Minimal beginnings even though his new work evolved from them. Describing his work in 1966, Stella stated, "My painting is based on the fact that only what can be seen there *is* there. . . . What you see is what you see."[1] This last phrase, now legendary, can be applied to any phase of Stella's work, for his goal, much like Ellsworth Kelly's (despite the great differences in their art), has always been to create the most compelling visual experiences possible, whether minimal or maximal or somewhere in between.

Born in Malden, Massachusetts, Stella attended Phillips Academy and then Princeton University, where he studied art with William Seitz and became friends with Walter Darby Bannard and Michael Fried. He moved to New York City in 1958 and has lived and worked in the area ever since. At the end of 1959, Stella had his big break when his Black paintings were included in *Sixteen Americans* at the Museum of Modern Art. These were large paintings composed of parallel horizontal and vertical stripes in black enamel made with a housepainter's brush, with a thin margin of raw canvas between each stripe. The only major differences between the paintings were the shape and size of the support and the pattern of stripes. Stella explained that the format "forces illusionistic space out of the painting at a constant rate by using a regulated pattern."[2] During the 1960s, he completed several series, including the Aluminum paintings, Copper paintings, Benjamin Moore paintings, Concentric Squares, and Mitered Mazes.

Flin Flon IV, named after a town in Canada, is from the Saskatchewan series, sixteen paintings created between 1967 and 1969, when Stella was teaching in Saskatchewan. The series is an elaboration of the Protractor series, in which Stella created monumental shaped canvases based on the curving forms of the protractor with interweaving bands of bright color. The Saskatchewan series adapts the Protractors to a square format. *Flin Flon IV* is structured around four overlapping semicircles that extend from each corner of the canvas through the center to suggest a quatrefoil design. The "IV" in the title reflects the fact that Stella executed multiple paintings (more than fifteen) titled *Flin Flon* within the larger series, each with a different, intuitively determined color scheme. Spatial illusion is reduced by the flat application of color but reinstated by the system of overlaps. In 1963, Stella had traveled to Iran, where he became fascinated with Islamic architecture: "There's all that interlacing, or interweaving. . . . Things doubling back on themselves, like snakes swallowing their tails. This came out in the Protractor pictures."[3] Around this time, Stella studied the work of Henri Matisse, whose embrace of decorative pattern is reflected in *Flin Flon IV*.

Chodorow II belongs to the Polish Village series of 1970–1973, a group of more than 130 works. Stella named the works after Polish synagogues built between the seventeenth and nineteenth centuries that were destroyed by Adolf Hitler during World War II. The artist had learned about them from *Wooden Synagogues* (1959), a book that included photographs of the synagogues taken in the 1920s and 1930s in a Constructivist style using sharply angled viewpoints.[4] Stella began with preparatory drawings, which he then used to create models out of cardboard. The full-size paintings were realized in two versions: the first used felt, paper, and paint and resembled giant collages; the second used thicker materials including Masonite and plywood affixed to wood in relief. The

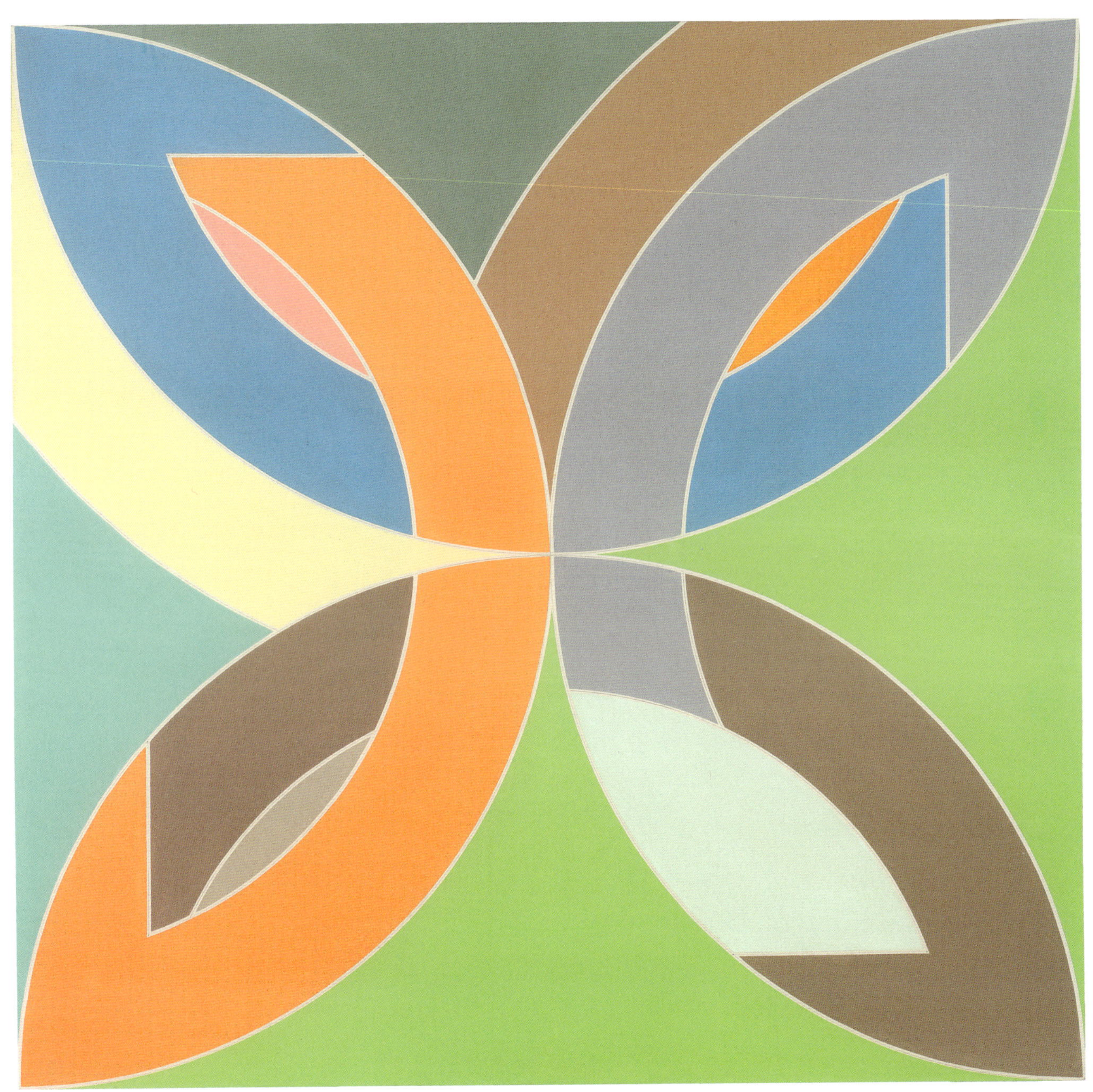

41. Frank Stella, *Flin Flon IV*, 1969. Polymer and fluorescent polymer paint on canvas, 96 1/2 x 96 1/2 in. (245.1 x 245.1 cm). 1994.82.1

Chodorow set is unique because it was executed in five versions. In all its variations, the series reflects Stella's interest in architectural plans, Russian Constructivism, and Synthetic Cubism, and it paves the way for an increasing degree of relief in Stella's work as his "paintings" leave the wall to enter our space.

La scienza della fiacca (4x), translated as "The Science of Laziness," comes from the Cones and Pillars series, made between 1984 and 1987, forty-eight metal reliefs, each named after a story in Italo Calvino's *Italian Folktales* (1956). Describing the series, Stella said:

> The Cones and Pillars have a blunt, primitive quality to them as paintings. . . . They have very much the spirit of the well-told folktale. They are very active, they're very fantasy-like, and they're very simple—even brutal—in the way that fairy tales are. . . . I had the feeling that with a little bit of mental jockeying their forms could represent things. It wasn't hard to imagine them being a cat or a person.[5]

This particular example is defined by three overlapping, schematic depictions of cylinders at left, each rendered in stripes of different colors—black and white, bright pink and blue, yellow and brown. Unlike the other two, the top cylinder angles toward the wall. A fourth partial cylinder can just be discerned at right, interrupted by a jigsaw shape covered with gestural brushstrokes that gives the appearance of being above it. On top of this piece, in turn, lies the most dramatic element of the work, the sharply pointed image of a lined cone, which directs our attention back to the center.

As he did in many of his later works, Stella carefully planned this one in advance; it was created at a workshop and then returned to his studio for him to paint. The process resembles sculpture fabrication, and the results have strongly sculptural elements, yet, crucially, the work hangs on the wall. Stella insists that in such works he is a painter: "The impulse that goes into them is pictorial, and they live or die on my pictorial abilities, not my abilities as a sculptor."[6]

PR

---

1 Frank Stella, quoted in Bruce Glaser, "Questions to Stella and Judd," ed. Lucy R. Lippard, *ARTnews* 65, no. 5 (September 1966): 58–59.

2 From Stella's lecture at Pratt Institute in January or February 1960, quoted in William Rubin, *Frank Stella, 1970–1987*, exh. cat. (New York: Museum of Modern Art, 1987), 22.

3 Stella, quoted in Calvin Tomkins, "Profiles: The Space Around Real Things," *New Yorker*, September 10, 1984, 84.

4 See Mark Godfrey, *Abstraction and the Holocaust* (New Haven, CT, and London: Yale University Press, 2007), 79–111.

5 Stella, quoted in Rubin, *Frank Stella*, 142.

6 Stella, quoted in Roger Kimball, "Frank Stella," *New Criterion* 6, no. 4 (December 1987): 26.

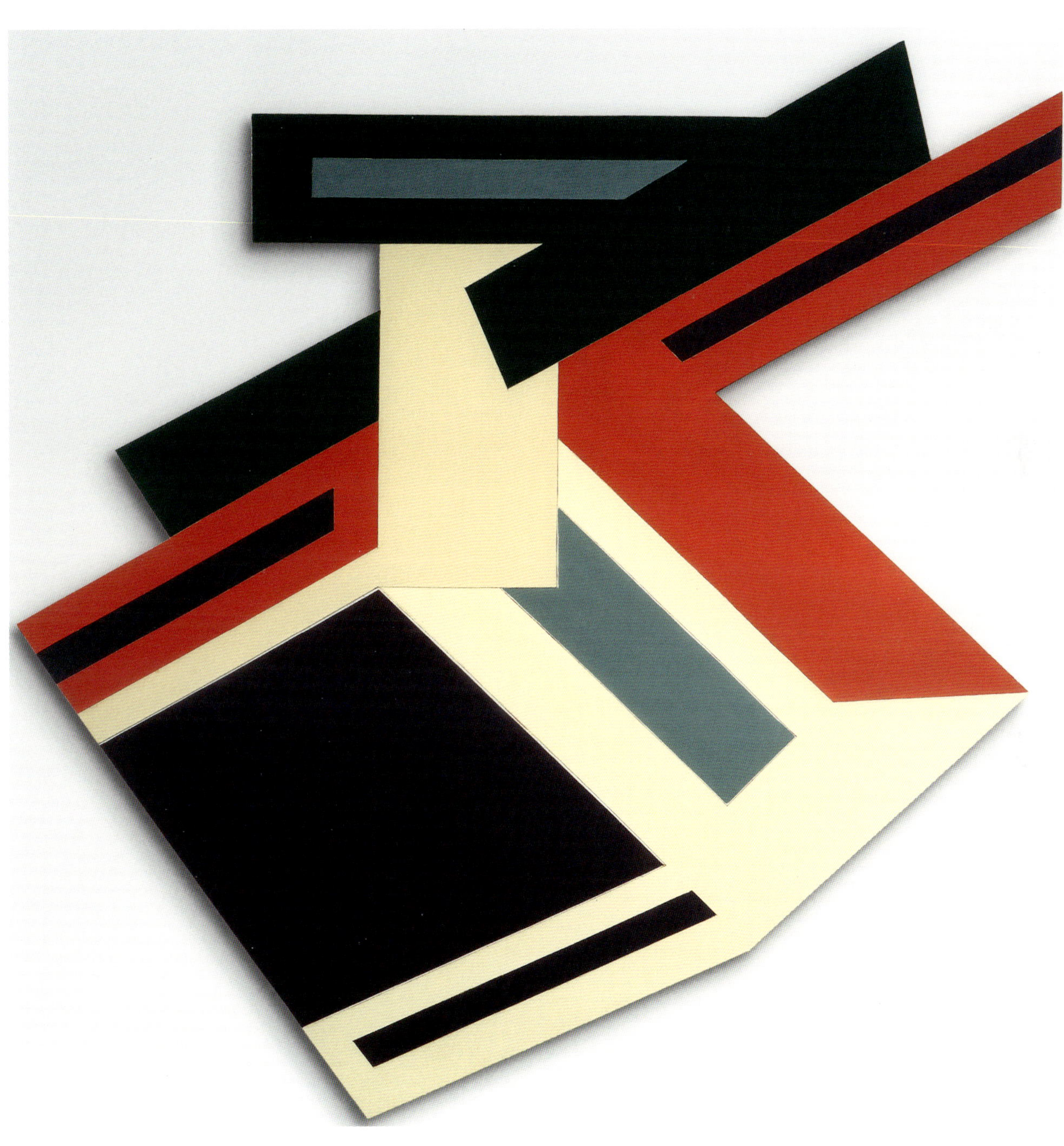

42. Frank Stella, *Chodorow II*, 1971. Felt, paper, and canvas collage on canvas, 108 1/8 x 106 in. (274.4 x 269.3 cm). 1992.28.5

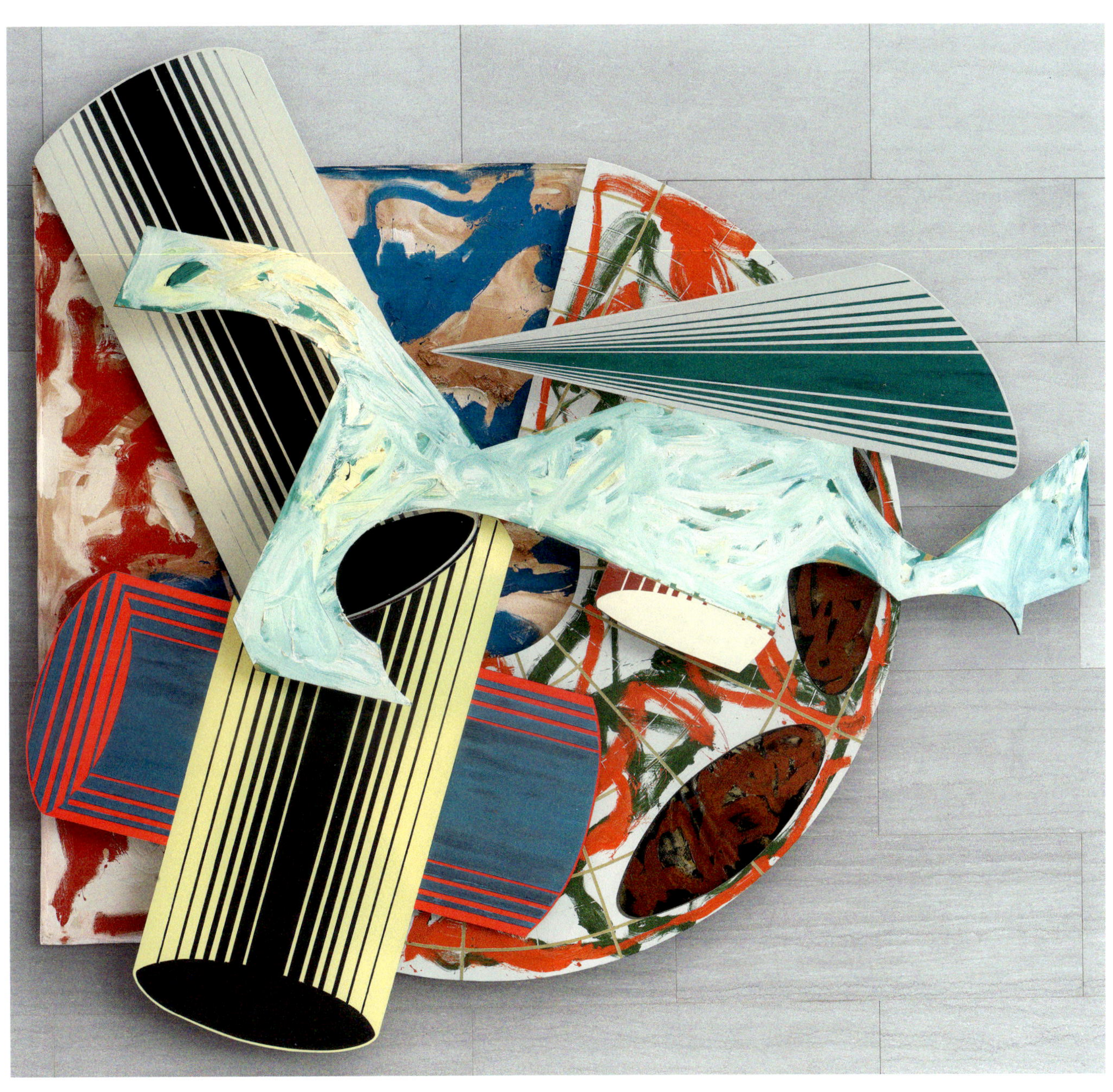

43. Frank Stella, *La scienza della fiacca (4x)*, 1984. Oil, urethane enamel, fluorescent alkyd paint, acrylic, and printing ink on canvas, etched magnesium, aluminum, and fiberglass, 143 x 151 x 30 in. (363.2 x 383.5 x 76.2 cm). 1995.79.2

CLYFFORD STILL

AMERICAN, 1904–1980

A founder of Abstract Expressionism, Clyfford Still is the least-known member of that pioneering group. Jackson Pollock, the best known, once said, "Still makes the rest of us look academic."[1] Many others, from Mark Rothko to Robert Motherwell to Clement Greenberg, hailed Still's originality.[2] But his fortunes suffered a self-inflicted blow when he retreated from the art world in the early 1950s and proceeded to hold on to the vast majority of his work, refusing most sales and exhibitions until his death in 1980. With the opening of the Clyfford Still Museum in Denver in 2011, his full achievement is gradually coming to light.[3]

Born in North Dakota, Still grew up in Washington State and Alberta, Canada, where he did farmwork under a brutal father during the Dust Bowl. He attended Spokane University and received his MFA in 1935 from Washington State with a thesis on the art of Paul Cézanne. After moving to California in 1941, he had a solo exhibition at the San Francisco Museum of Art in 1943 and met Rothko, who was teaching there. When Still moved to New York in 1945, Rothko introduced him to Peggy Guggenheim, who gave him a show at her Art of This Century Gallery. Still taught at the California School of Fine Arts in the late 1940s, returned to New York in 1950, and then continued to move around the country taking various academic jobs. In 1961, he finally settled on a farm in rural Maryland, where he lived and painted until his death.

Filled with gaunt, tortured-looking farmers and their families, Still's early works have been called "pastorals from hell."[4] A talented draftsman, Still "de-skilled" by abandoning brushes around 1927 in favor of the palette knife, which he used for the remainder of his career. By the late 1930s, he had distilled the human figure to an upright cipher, or what he called a "lifeline."[5] His art developed quickly in California in the mid-1940s, and by 1947 he had arrived at his characteristic abstract style: fields of color with jagged outlines and rough surfaces created by dragging paint with the knife, resulting in what Greenberg described memorably as "frayed leaf and spread-hide contours."[6] Accordingly, Still abandoned descriptive titles in favor of a system of numbers and letters.

Still's mature paintings tend to follow one of three patterns: some (especially the later works) include large areas of unpainted canvas; in others, color fields are punctuated by one or two dramatic vertical accents; and a third type includes few incidents at all and approaches monochrome. With its attenuated, intermittent lifeline, *1951–N* sits somewhere between the latter two.[7] A wall of earthy burnt sienna is cut by crimson streaks, with an accent of yellow at the top edge and a sliver of ultramarine at the bottom right (which appears intermittently from beneath the sienna field). In several areas, the sienna wall gives way almost imperceptibly to a smoother underlayer of lighter brown. The knifed surface at once evokes violent action and hardened rock, as if a current of force has been petrified.[8] In this context, the outbursts of primary color embody pure otherness, suggesting a dramatic struggle between the earthen field and glimmers of light. Robert Rosenblum has connected Still's work, along with Rothko's, to a Romantic tradition of depicting nature as sublime and terrifying.[9] It is tempting to read Still's paintings as apocalyptic, and difficult to ignore the artist's suggestion that his works aspire to embody the cycle "of the Earth, the Damned, and of the Recreated."[10]

KR

---

1 Jackson Pollock, quoted in Sam Hunter, *Masters of the Fifties: American Abstract Painting from Pollock to Stella* (New York: Marisa del Re Gallery, 1985), n.p. The quote comes from Hunter's account of a conversation with Pollock.

2 For more on Still's admirers and detractors, see David Anfam, "Clyfford Still's Art: Between the Quick and the Dead," in *Clyfford Still*, exh. cat. (Washington, DC: Hirshhorn Museum and Sculpture Garden in association with Yale University Press, 2001), 18–19. See also John Golding, *Paths to the Absolute: Mondrian, Malevich, Kandinsky, Pollock, Newman, Rothko, and Still* (London: Thames & Hudson, 2002), 200.

3 David Anfam argues that by the end of the twentieth century Still was "in near total eclipse" in his essay "Still's Journey," in Dean Sobel and David Anfam, *Clyfford Still: The Artist's Museum* (New York: Skira Rizzoli, 2012), 59.

4 Ibid., 70.

5 Thomas Albright, "A Conversation with Clyfford Still," *ARTnews* 75 (March 1976): 34. Albright asserts that Still referred to the vertical element as a lifeline. In a May 1976 letter to the editor, Still corrected a few of Albright's assertions but not this one.

6 Clement Greenberg, "'American-Type' Painting," in *Art and Culture: Critical Essays* (Boston: Beacon Press, 1961), 224.

7 David Anfam in *Art for the Nation: Gifts in Honor of the 50th Anniversary of the National Gallery of Art*, exh. cat. (Washington, DC: National Gallery of Art, 1991), 394.

8 David Anfam, "Clyfford Still," in Mark Rosenthal, ed., *The Robert and Jane Meyerhoff Collection: 1945–1995*, exh. cat. (Washington, DC: National Gallery of Art, 1996), 223.

9 Robert Rosenblum, *Modern Painting and the Northern Romantic Tradition: Friedrich to Rothko* (New York: HarperCollins, 1977).

10 Still, quoted in Mark Rothko, *First Exhibition: Paintings, Clyfford Still*, exh. cat. (New York: Art of This Century, 1946), n.p. See also David Anfam, "'Of the Earth, the Damned, and of the Recreated': Aspects of Clyfford Still's Earlier Work," *Burlington Magazine* 135 (April 1993): 260–269.

44. Clyfford Still, *1951–N*, 1951. Oil on canvas, 92 3/8 x 69 1/8 in. (234.5 x 175.6 cm).
Gift in Honor of the 50th Anniversary of the National Gallery of Art. 1989.87.1

BRADLEY WALKER TOMLIN

AMERICAN, 1899–1953

Despite a short career, Bradley Walker Tomlin left behind an original oeuvre that combined the bold gestures of Abstract Expressionism with quiet lyricism and a Cubist structure. In the words of Duncan Phillips, one of his patrons, "He was ever the musician striving to bring order out of complexity or to elaborate a simple melody with subtle variations."[1]

Born in Syracuse, New York, Tomlin studied art at Syracuse University and began his career working in New York City as an illustrator for Condé Nast publications. During the late 1920s, he adopted the style of the Precisionists, whose realism was defined by sharp geometries; later he turned to a version of Cubism. He studied art in France, pursued portrait commissions, and got through the Depression by teaching art. In 1945, Tomlin met Adolph Gottlieb and joined the emerging circle of Abstract Expressionists, which also included Jackson Pollock, Robert Motherwell, and Philip Guston. It was in this potentially daunting context that he found his own voice: he moved toward freer forms and more spontaneous expression, experimenting with automatism and abandoning color for a time. Tomlin's last works reflect a growing assurance and ambition in his career, which was cut short by his death from a heart attack at age fifty-four.

Maneuver for Position marks Tomlin's transition from Cubist structures to more gestural work. What seem to be eyes scattered throughout the image recall series such as Gottlieb's Pictographs and Joan Miró's Constellations, the latter of which had recently been shown in New York. These ocular shapes are surrounded by accents of bold color. Drawn with white strokes, energetic ribbonlike arcs (reminiscent of the work of Paul Klee) maneuver across the canvas. The title of the painting has military connotations, no doubt alluding to the recent World War, but it can also be read as a reflection on Tomlin's own career, which involved a transatlantic negotiation of styles. The signature at lower center is one that Tomlin had recently adopted; its dashing quality declares new energy while its lowercase letters reflect a personality of quiet originality.[2]

PR

---

[1] Duncan Phillips, quoted in John I. H. Bauer, *Bradley Walker Tomlin* (New York: Macmillan, 1957), 13.

[2] David Bourdon, "In Praise of Bradley Walker Tomlin," *Art in America* 63, no. 5 (September–October 1975): 58.

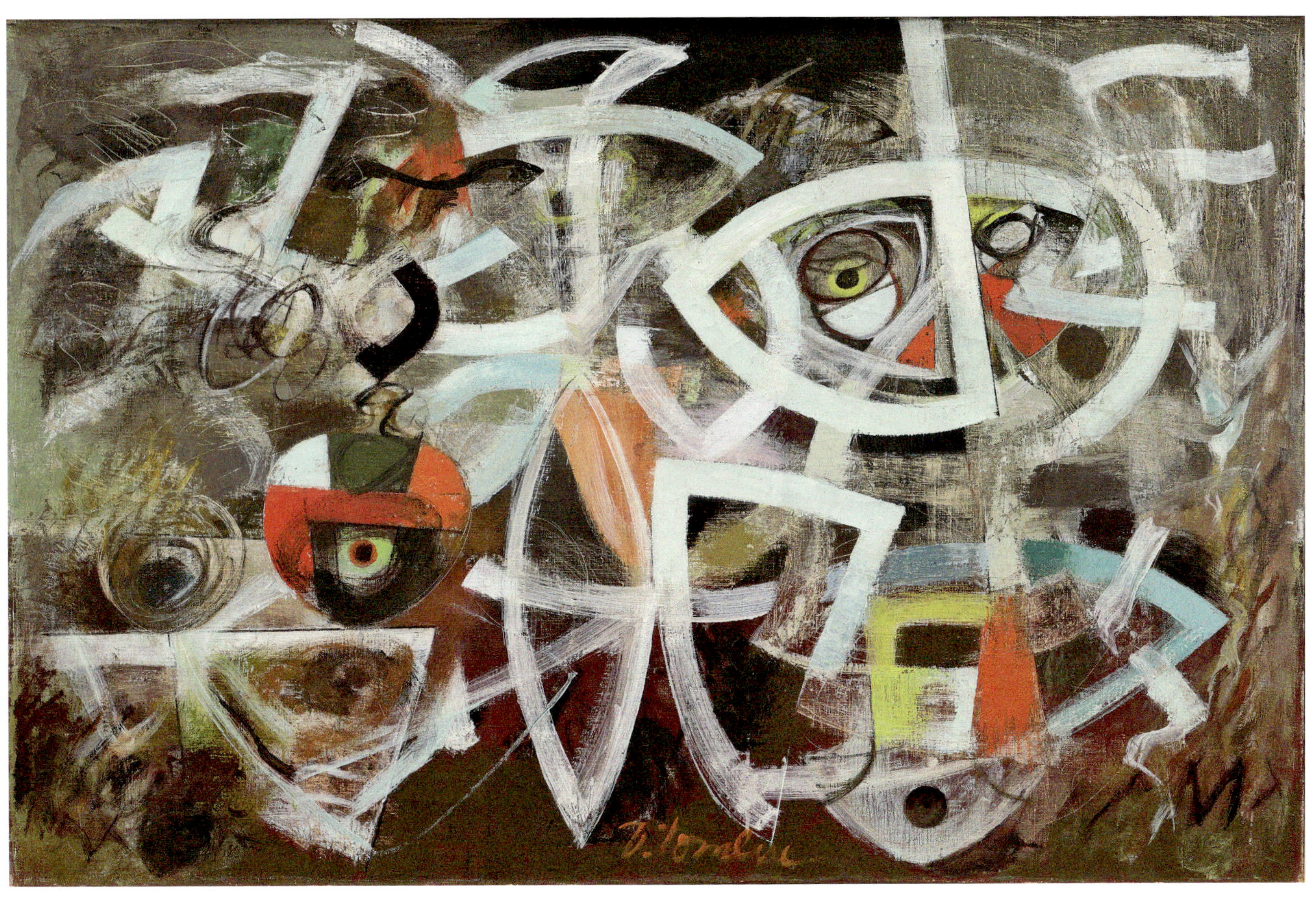

45. Bradley Walker Tomlin, *Maneuver for Position*, 1947. Oil on canvas, 31 x 46 in. (78.7 x 116.8 cm). 1996.81.2

TERRY WINTERS

AMERICAN, b. 1949

A prodigious painter, draftsman, and printmaker, Terry Winters has pushed the boundaries of art while maintaining a keen sense of its history and craft. Born in Brooklyn in 1949, he received a BFA in 1971 from Pratt Institute in New York. Although he first painted in a reductive style influenced by Minimalism, by the end of the 1970s he had allowed figuration into his work. He found early success with a solo exhibition at Sonnabend Gallery in 1982, followed quickly by exhibitions at major European and American museums. Through the 1980s, he explored such natural processes as crystal formation, fungal growth, and cellular division, usually rendered in a lush painterly manner. Since the 1990s, his paintings have typically emerged from a process of repurposing, abstracting, and overlaying imagery drawn from such diverse sources as medical photographs, weather maps, statistical charts, and computer graphics.

Graphics Tablet is one of a group of nine large paintings made between 1997 and 1999 that Winters called Graphic Primitives. The series parallels a group of nine black and white woodcuts of the same name. In *Graphics Tablet*, multi-colored painterly shapes form coffered patterns that overlap one another to create a complex network that spans the surface of the canvas. The network seems organized around a central fissure that splits the canvas from top to bottom, perhaps a visual analogue to the corpus callosum, a bundle of fibers that delivers messages between the cerebral hemispheres. This association, together with the suggestion of traffic patterns and city blocks, prompted John Rajchman to dub this imagery "the brain-city," but such a reading risks becoming literal and static.[1] Indeed, any visual unity or referential stability in *Graphics Tablet* is constantly undermined by the swarming activity of individual abstract units.

For Rajchman, the Graphic Primitives replaced the "window through which one sees, or the frame within which one locates," with "the table of information in which things slide back and forth, images arising from other images rather than from external things."[2] This seems especially relevant to *Graphics Tablet*: a graphics tablet is a computer input device that enables a user to draw images by hand using a stylus. Yet for all of Winters's interest in technology, his paintings remain insistently handmade. Similarly, despite his use of preliminary drawings and projected images, he always changes course on the canvas. In this he remains a die-hard modernist, one who has closely studied the work of Paul Cézanne, Jackson Pollock, and Piet Mondrian, among others. Winters explained his methodology: "My approach is to build a series of improvisational responses, a set of operating procedures . . . not a strict timetable, but a practice, like a musical practice."[3]

KR

---

1 John Rajchman, "Painting in the Brain-City," in *Terry Winters: Graphic Primitives*, exh. cat. (New York: Matthew Marks Gallery, 1999), 10.

2 Ibid., 7.

3 Winters, quoted in Adam Fuss, "Conversation with Terry Winters," in *Terry Winters: Computation of Chains*, exh. cat. (New York: Matthew Marks Gallery, 1997), 7.

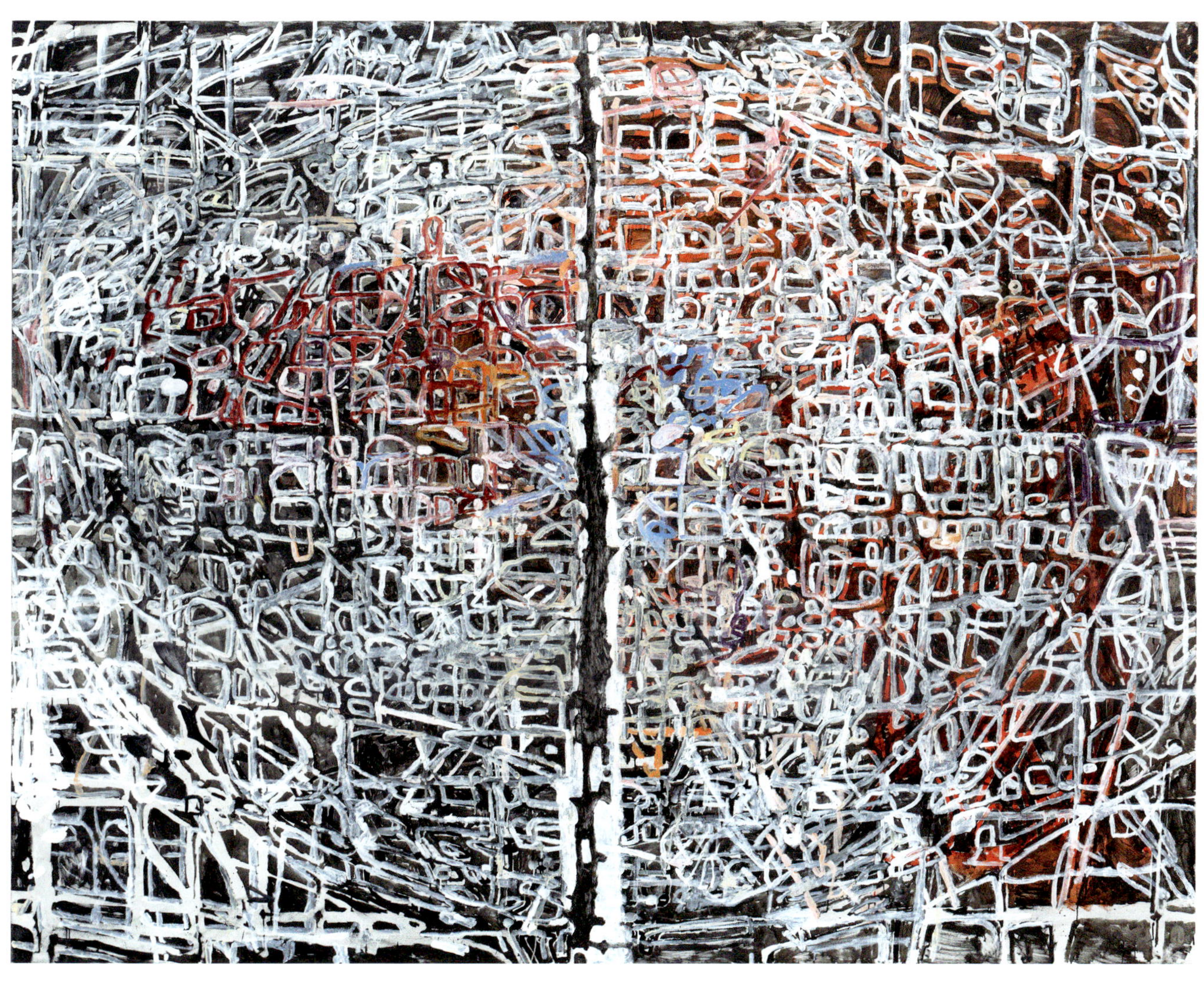

46. Terry Winters, *Graphics Tablet*, 1998. Oil and alkyd resin on canvas, 96 x 120 in. (243.8 x 304.8 cm). Collection of Robert and Jane Meyerhoff

SELECTED BIBLIOGRAPHY

Anfam, David. *Abstract Expressionism.* London: Thames & Hudson, 1990.

Clark, T. J. *Farewell to an Idea: Episodes from a History of Modernism.* New Haven, CT: Yale University Press, 1999.

Cooper, Harry. *The Robert and Jane Meyerhoff Collection: Selected Works.* Exh. cat. Washington, DC: National Gallery of Art, 2009.

Crow, Thomas. *The Rise of the Sixties: American and European Art in the Era of Dissent.* New Haven, CT: Yale University Press, 2005.

Foster, Hal. *The First Pop Age: Painting and Subjectivity in the Art of Hamilton, Lichtenstein, Warhol, Richter, and Ruscha.* Princeton: Princeton University Press, 2011.

Foster, Hal, Rosalind Krauss, Yve-Alain Bois, and Benjamin H. D. Buchloh. *Art since 1900: Modernism, Antimodernism, Postmodernism.* 2nd ed. 2 vols. London: Thames & Hudson, 2011.

Frascina, Francis, ed. *Pollock and After: The Critical Debate.* 2nd ed. London and New York: Routledge, 2000.

Frascina, Francis, and Charles Harrison, eds. *Modern Art and Modernism: A Critical Anthology.* New York: Harper & Row, 1982.

Fried, Michael. *Art and Objecthood: Essays and Reviews.* Chicago and London: University of Chicago Press, 1998.

Golding, John. *Paths to the Absolute: Mondrian, Malevich, Kandinsky, Pollock, Newman, Rothko, and Still.* Princeton: Princeton University Press, 2000.

Greenberg, Clement. *Art and Culture: Critical Essays.* Boston: Beacon Press, 1961.

Guilbaut, Serge, ed. *Reconstructing Modernism: Art in New York, Paris, and Montreal, 1945–1964.* Cambridge, MA: MIT Press, 1992.

Harrison, Charles, and Paul Wood, eds. *Art in Theory, 1900–1990: An Anthology of Changing Ideas.* Oxford: Blackwell, 1992.

Hughes, Robert. *The Shock of the New: The Hundred-Year History of Modern Art—Its Rise, Its Dazzling Achievement, Its Fall.* New York: Alfred A. Knopf, 1991.

Jones, Caroline A. *Machine in the Studio: Constructing the Postwar American Artist.* Chicago: University of Chicago Press, 1998.

Krauss, Rosalind E. *The Optical Unconscious.* Cambridge, MA: MIT Press, 1993.

Leja, Michael. *Reframing Abstract Expressionism: Subjectivity and Painting in the 1940s.* New Haven, CT: Yale University Press, 1997.

Mattison, Robert Saltonstall. *Masterworks in the Robert & Jane Meyerhoff Collection: Jasper Johns, Robert Rauschenberg, Roy Lichtenstein, Ellsworth Kelly, Frank Stella.* New York: Hudson Hills Press, 1995.

O'Doherty, Brian. *American Masters: The Voice and the Myth in Modern Art.* New York: Random House, 1982.

Polcari, Stephen. *Abstract Expressionism and the Modern Experience.* Cambridge: Cambridge University Press, 1993.

Rosenberg, Harold. *The Tradition of the New.* New York: Grove Press, 1961.

Rosenthal, Mark, ed. *The Robert and Jane Meyerhoff Collection: 1945–1995.* Exh. cat. Washington, DC: National Gallery of Art, 1996.

Sandler, Irving. *The Triumph of American Painting: A History of Abstract Expressionism.* New York: Harper & Row, 1976.

Schapiro, Meyer. *Modern Art, 19th and 20th Centuries: Selected Papers.* New York: George Braziller, 1978.

Steinberg, Leo. *Other Criteria: Confrontations with Twentieth-Century Art.* New York: Oxford University Press, 1972.

Sundell, Nina C., ed. *The Robert and Jane Meyerhoff Collection: 1958–1979.* Baltimore: Baltimore Museum of Art, 1980.

Sylvester, David. *Interviews with American Artists.* New Haven, CT: Yale University Press, 2001.

Varnedoe, Kirk. *Pictures of Nothing: Abstract Art since Pollock.* Princeton: Princeton University Press, 2006.

ACKNOWLEDGMENTS

This exhibition and publication would not have been possible without the generous partnership of the National Gallery of Art, Washington. I thank Earl A. Powell III, director, for his support of this project, and Harry Cooper, curator and head of modern art, for his myriad contributions, including the vibrant texts he wrote for this book. Gratitude is extended to the other catalogue authors from the National Gallery: Molly Donovan, James Meyer, Jennifer Roberts, Kerry Rose, and Paige Rozanski, all members of the Department of Modern Art. Thanks are further extended to Franklin Kelly, deputy director and chief curator, and Dodge Thompson, chief of exhibitions. Essential contributions were made by Michelle Fondas, head registrar, and her team; Jay Krueger, chief of paintings conservation; Lisa MacDougall, head of loan services; Nancy Breuer, deputy general counsel; Alan Newman, head of imaging and visual services, and his team, including Peter Huestis; and all of those who ensured the safe transport and optimal display of the artworks.

At the Fine Arts Museums of San Francisco, I thank Diane B. Wilsey, president of the Board of Trustees, for her enthusiasm, and Colin B. Bailey, director of museums, for his support. Thanks are also extended to Julian Cox, founding curator of photography and chief administrative curator; Timothy Anglin Burgard, Ednah Root Curator in Charge of American Art; Michele Gutierrez-Canepa, chief financial officer and foundation fiscal officer; and Suzy Peterson, executive assistant in the art division. Appreciation is given to the Museums' exhibitions team: Krista Brugnara, director of exhibitions; Therese Chen, director of collections management; Craig Harris, manager of installation and preparation; and Daniel Meza, graphic design director. I am also grateful to Sheila Pressley, director of education; Renee Baldocchi, director of public programs; and Maureen Keefe, director of marketing and communications.

This publication was overseen by Leslie Dutcher, director of publications, who managed it with grace. Thanks are also extended to Laura Harger and Danica Michels Hodge, editors. I also thank Kathryn Shedrick for her editorial contributions; Yolanda de Montijo, Frank Kofsuske, and Georgina Lee at Em Dash for their elegant design; Sue Medlicott, Nerissa Vales, and Michelle Woo at the Production Department for their expertise; and Massimo Tonolli and his colleagues at Trifolio for their luminous printing of this book. I am further grateful to the Andrew W. Mellon Foundation Endowment for Publications, which has made this catalogue possible.

An undertaking of this magnitude, of course, would not be possible without the generous support of our patrons and the many foundations that assist us in our presentations. I thank Penny and James George Coulter, the Estate of Dr. Charles L. Dibble, the Bernard Osher Foundation, the Lisa and Douglas Goldman Fund, the National Endowment for the Arts, Lorna Meyer Calas and Dennis Calas, Nion T. McEvoy, Richard and Peggy Greenfield, and the Ednah Root Foundation. I further thank the Federal Council on the Arts and the Humanities for their support.

These acknowledgments would not be complete without recognizing the artists whose work is included in the exhibition and this volume. I am grateful to their studios, estates, foundations, and representatives, whose kind cooperation has enabled us to showcase their talents. My warmest gratitude, however, must be given to Robert Meyerhoff, who, with his late wife, Jane, built this remarkable collection and has shared it so generously with the National Gallery of Art and, by extension, with our Museums.

Richard Benefield
Deputy Director, Fine Arts Museums of San Francisco

INDEX OF ARTISTS AND ARTWORKS

This index contains all of the artists represented in the exhibition *Modernism from the National Gallery of Art: The Robert and Jane Meyerhoff Collection*. Page numbers in **bold** refer to illustrations.

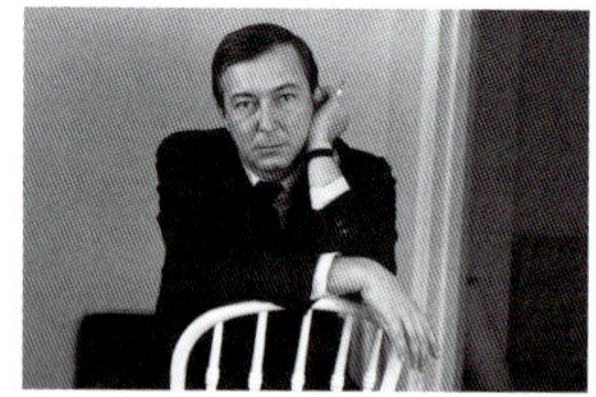

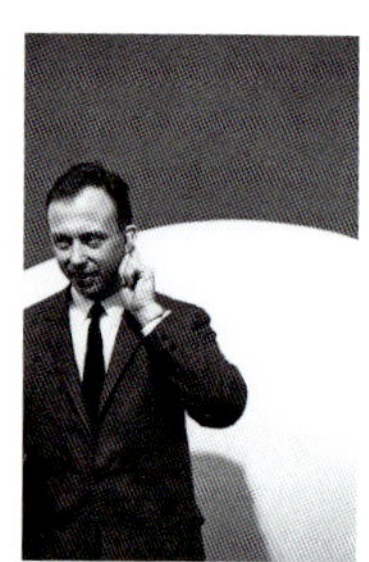

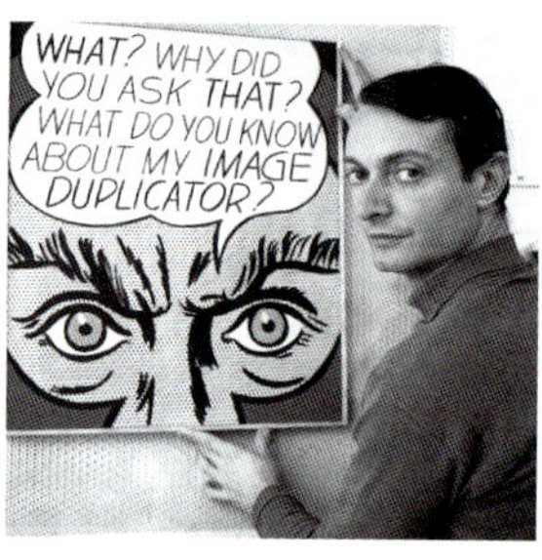
WHAT? WHY DID YOU ASK THAT? WHAT DO YOU KNOW ABOUT MY IMAGE DUPLICATOR?

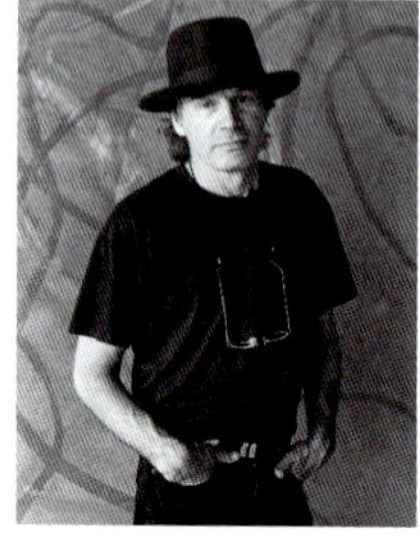

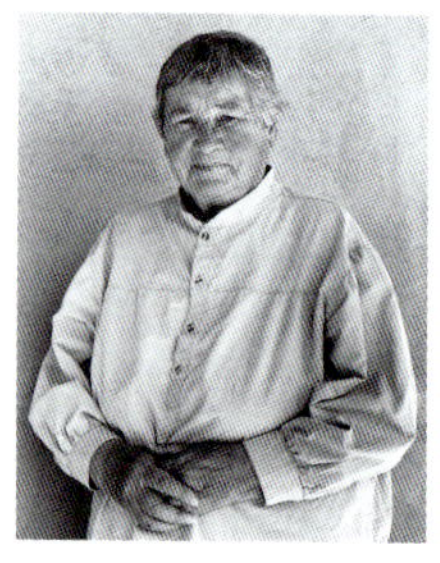

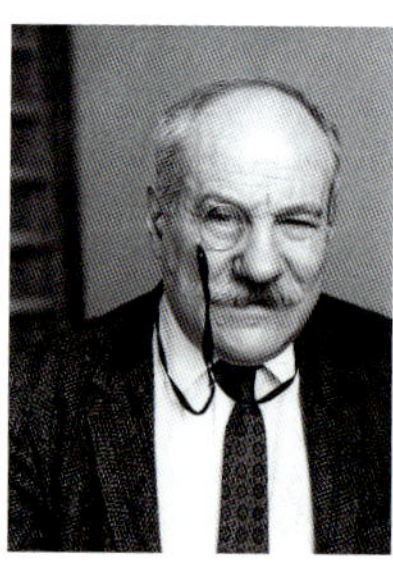

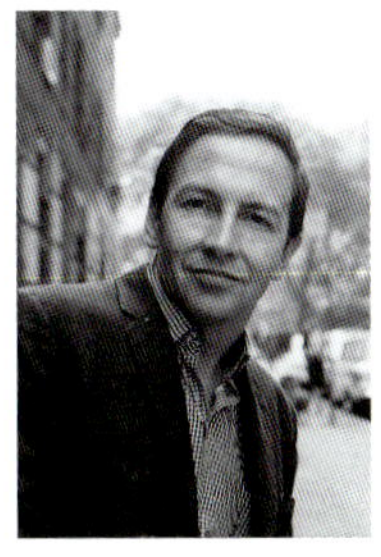

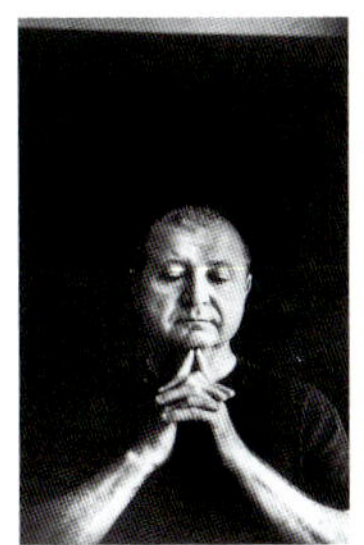

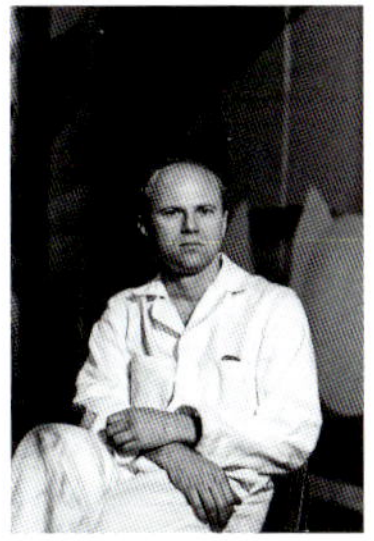

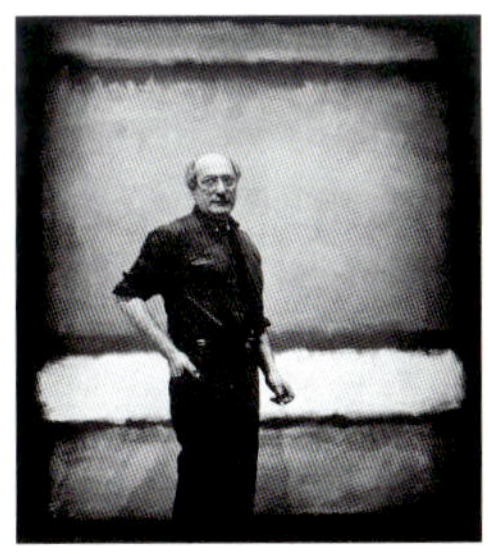

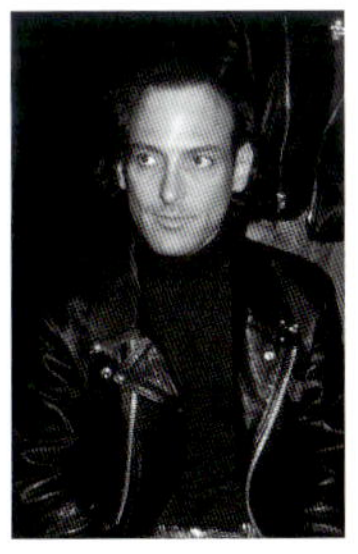

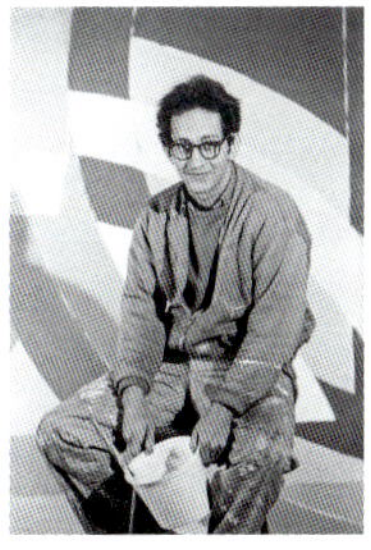

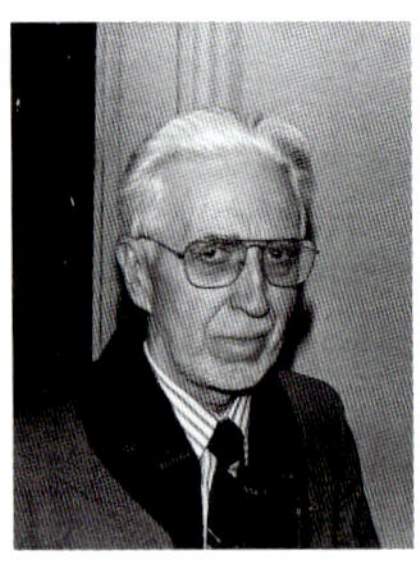

CLYFFORD STILL

American, 1904–1980

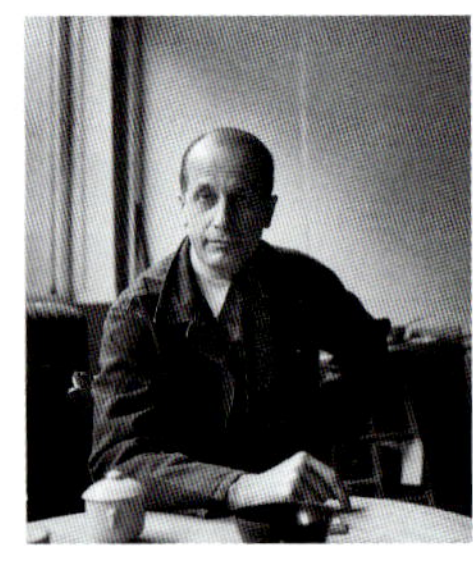

BRADLEY WALKER TOMLIN

American, 1899–1953

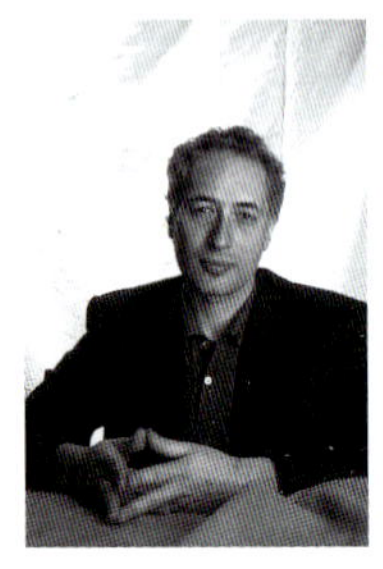

TERRY WINTERS

American, b. 1949

PHOTOGRAPHY CREDITS FOR INDEX

Josef Albers: photograph by Barbara Morgan, 1944. Barbara Morgan / Getty Images. William Baziotes: photograph by Fred W. McDarrah, 1962. Fred W. McDarrah / Getty Images. Anthony Caro: photograph by Tony Evans, ca. 1965. Tony Evans / Timelapse Library Ltd. / Getty Images. Joseph Cornell: photograph by David Gahr, 1967. The Estate of David Gahr / Getty Images. Burgoyne Diller: photograph by Walter Rosenblum, n.d. Walter Rosenblum Collection, Smithsonian American Art Museum, R0000306. Jean Dubuffet: unidentified photographer, 1943. Apic / Getty Images. Eric Fischl: photograph by Oliver Morris, ca. 1985. Oliver Morris / Getty Images. Nancy Graves: photograph by Bernbard Gotfryd, 1973. Bernard Gotfryd / Getty Images. Philip Guston: photograph by Fred W. McDarrah, ca. 1960. Fred W. McDarrah / Getty Images. Grace Hartigan: photograph by Fred W. McDarrah, 1960. Fred W. McDarrah / Getty Images. Howard Hodgkin: photograph by Tony Evans, ca. 1965. Tony Evans / Timelapse Library Ltd. / Getty Images. Hans Hofmann: photograph by Fred W. McDarrah, 1961. Fred W. McDarrah / Getty Images. Jasper Johns: photograph by David Gahr, 1966. The Estate of David Gahr / Getty Images. Ellsworth Kelly: photograph by Fred W. McDarrah, 1963. Fred W. McDarrah / Getty Images. Roy Lichtenstein: photograph by Mondadori, 1959. Mondadori / Getty Images. Brice Marden: photograph by Chris Felver, 1994. Chris Felver / Getty Images. Agnes Martin: photograph by Chris Felver, 1994. Chris Felver / Getty Images. Barnett Newman: photograph by Fred W. McDarrah, 1961. Fred W. McDarrah / Getty Images. Robert Rauschenberg: photograph by David Gahr, 1965. The Estate of David Gahr / Getty Images. Ad Reinhardt: photograph by John Loengard, ca. 1966. John Loengard / Getty Images. James Rosenquist: photograph by David Gahr, 1965. The Estate of David Gahr / Getty Images. Mark Rothko: photograph by Kate Rothko, 1961. Apic / Getty Images. David Salle: photograph by Rose Hartman, 2003. Rose Hartman / Getty Images. Frank Stella: photograph by David Gahr, 1967. The Estate of David Gahr / Getty Images. Clyfford Still: photograph by Fred W. McDarrah, 1978. Fred W. McDarrah / Getty Images. Bradley Walker Tomlin: photograph by Kay Bell Reynal, 1952. Archives of American Art, Smithsonian Institution. Terry Winters: photograph by Ted Thai, 1986. Ted Thai / Getty Images.

PICTURE CREDITS

All artworks in the collection of the National Gallery of Art, Washington, are courtesy of the National Gallery of Art, Washington, unless otherwise noted.

Figure artworks: p. 12: Bill Wilson, National Gallery of Art, Washington, DC, Gallery Archives. p. 13: Lee Ewing, National Gallery of Art, Washington, DC, Gallery Archives. Fig. 1: © RMN-Grand Palais / Art Resource, NY. Figs. 3 and 7: © 2014 Renate, Hans & Maria Hofmann Trust / Artists Rights Society (ARS), New York. Fig. 4: © 2014 The Josef and Anni Albers Foundation / Artists Rights Society (ARS), New York. Fig. 5: Courtesy Mildred Lane Kemper Art Museum, Washington University, Saint Louis. Fig. 6: © Succession H. Matisse / Artists Rights Society (ARS), New York. Digital Image © The Museum of Modern Art / Licensed by SCALA / Art Resource, NY. Fig. 8: Art © Jasper Johns / Licensed by VAGA, New York, NY. Fig. 9: Art © Robert Rauschenberg Foundation / Licensed by VAGA, New York, NY. Fig. 10: © 2014 The Barnett Newman Foundation, New York: Artists Rights Society (ARS), New York. Digital Image © The Museum of Modern Art / Licensed by SCALA / Art Resource, NY. Fig. 11: © Paul Katz. Paul Katz Archive, Department of Image Collections, National Gallery of Art Library, Washington, DC. Fig. 12: © 2014 The Barnett Newman Foundation, New York: Artists Rights Society (ARS), New York. Fig. 13: © Succession H. Matisse / Artists Rights Society (ARS), New York. © RMN-Grand Palais / Art Resource, NY.

Plate artworks: Pls. 1–15 and pp. 32–33: © 2014 The Barnett Newman Foundation, New York: Artists Rights Society (ARS), New York. Pl. 16 and p. 4: © 2014 The Josef and Anni Albers Foundation / Artists Rights Society (ARS), New York. Pl. 17: © Estate of William Baziotes. Pl. 18: © Barford Sculptures Ltd., courtesy Barford Sculptures. Pls. 19–20: Art © The Joseph and Robert Cornell Memorial Foundation / Licensed by VAGA, New York, NY. Pl. 21 and p. 8: Art © Estate of Burgoyne Diller / Licensed by VAGA, New York, NY. Pl. 22: © 2014 Artists Rights Society (ARS), New York / ADAGP, Paris. Pl. 23: Copyright Eric Fischl. Pl. 24: Art © Nancy Graves Foundation / Licensed by VAGA, New York, NY. Pl. 25: © Estate of Philip Guston; courtesy McKee Gallery. Pl. 26: Estate of Grace Hartigan; courtesy C. Grimaldis Gallery. Pl. 27: © Howard Hodgkin, courtesy Gagosian Gallery. Pl. 28 and p. 16: © 2014 Renate, Hans & Maria Hofmann Trust / Artists Rights Society (ARS), New York. Pl. 29: Art © Jasper Johns / Licensed by VAGA, New York, NY. Pl. 30: © Ellsworth Kelly. Pls. 31–32, p. 10, and cover: © Estate of Roy Lichtenstein. Pl. 33: © 2014 Brice Marden / Artists Rights Society (ARS), New York. Pl. 34: © 2014 Agnes Martin / Artists Rights Society (ARS), New York. Pl. 35: Art © Robert Rauschenberg Foundation / Licensed by VAGA, New York, NY. Pls. 36–37: © 2014 Estate of Ad Reinhardt / Artists Rights Society (ARS), New York. Pl. 38: Art © James Rosenquist / Licensed by VAGA, New York, NY. Pl. 39: © 1998 Kate Rothko Prizel & Christopher Rothko / Artists Rights Society (ARS), New York. Pl. 40: Art © David Salle / Licensed by VAGA, NY, NY. Courtesy of Mary Boone Gallery, NY. Pls. 41–43 and p. 6: © 2014 Frank Stella / Artists Rights Society (ARS), New York. Pl. 44: © Clyfford Still Estate, courtesy of Clyfford Still Museum, Denver, CO. Pl. 46: © Terry Winters, courtesy Matthew Marks Gallery.

This catalogue is published by the Fine Arts Museums of San Francisco on the occasion of the exhibition *Modernism from the National Gallery of Art: The Robert and Jane Meyerhoff Collection*:

de Young, San Francisco
June 7–October 12, 2014

This exhibition is organized by the National Gallery of Art, Washington, and the Fine Arts Museums of San Francisco.

Presenting Sponsors
Penny and James George Coulter

Director's Circle
Estate of Dr. Charles L. Dibble

President's Circle
The Bernard Osher Foundation

THE BERNARD
OSHER
FOUNDATION

Curator's Circle
Lisa and Douglas Goldman Fund

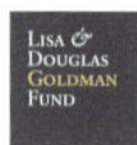

Conservator's Circle
National Endowment for the Arts

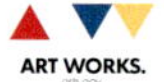

Benefactor's Circle
Lorna Meyer Calas and Dennis Calas
Nion T. McEvoy

Patron's Circle
Richard and Peggy Greenfield
Ednah Root Foundation

This catalogue is published with the assistance of the Andrew W. Mellon Foundation Endowment for Publications.

This exhibition is supported by an indemnity from the Federal Council on the Arts and the Humanities.

Picture credits are on pages 126 and 127.

Fine Arts Museums of San Francisco
de Young, Golden Gate Park
50 Hagiwara Tea Garden Drive
San Francisco, CA 94118-4502
www.famsf.org

Leslie Dutcher, Director of Publications
Laura Harger, Editor
Danica Michels Hodge, Editor

Edited by Kathryn Shedrick
Proofread by Susan Richmond
Photo research by Danica Michels Hodge and Lucy Medrich
Index by Andrew Joron
Designed and typeset by Yolanda de Montijo, Em Dash
Production management by The Production Department
Separations, printing, and binding by Trifolio Srl, Italy

Opening illustrations
p. 4: Josef Albers, *Study for Homage to the Square: Light Rising*, 1950, altered 1959 (pl. 16)
p. 6: Frank Stella, *Flin Flon IV*, 1969 (pl. 41)
p. 8: Burgoyne Diller, *First Theme*, 1964 (pl. 21)
p. 10: Roy Lichtenstein, *Painting with Statue of Liberty*, 1983 (pl. 32)
p. 16: Hans Hofmann, *Autumn Gold*, 1957 (pl. 28)

Cover art: Roy Lichtenstein, *Painting with Statue of Liberty*, 1983 (pl. 32). © Estate of Roy Lichtenstein

Library of Congress Cataloging-in-Publication Data

Modernism from the National Gallery of Art : the Robert and Jane Meyerhoff Collection / Harry Cooper, editor.

pages cm

"Published by the Fine Arts Museums of San Francisco on the occasion of the exhibition Modernism from the National Gallery of Art: The Robert and Jane Meyerhoff Collection, on view at the de Young museum, San Francisco, June 7, 2014–October 12, 2014."

Includes bibliographical references and index.

ISBN 978-0-88401-143-9 (hardcover : alk. paper)

1. Modernism (Art)—United States—Exhibitions. 2. Painting, American—20th century—Exhibitions. 3. Meyerhoff, Robert—Art collections—Exhibitions. 4. Meyerhoff, Jane—Art collections—Exhibitions. 5. Painting—Private collections—Washington (D.C.)—Exhibitions. 6. National Gallery of Art (U.S.)—Exhibitions. I. Cooper, Harry, 1959– editor. II. M.H. de Young Memorial Museum.

ND212.5.M63M63 2014

759.13'07479461—DC23

2014005923

ISBN 978-0-88401-143-9